# 40 | WHO IS JESUS?

**PICTURES TO SHARE WITH YOUR FAMILY**

BY **KATE HOX** ILLUSTRATED BY **JOE HOX**

NEW GROWTH PRESS

New Growth Press, Greensboro, NC 27401
Text Copyright © 2022 by Katherine Hoksbergen
Illustration Copyright © 2022 by Joseph Hoksbergen

Cover/Interior Design: Alecia Sharp

ISBN: 978-1-64507-229-4

Library of Congress Cataloging-in-Publication Data on File

Printed in India

29 28 27 26 25 24 23 22     1 2 3 4 5

# CONTENTS

# CONTENTS

*In loving memory of my dear mom,*
*Doris Jean Boer. This book would not exist*
*without your encouragement. We love you*
*and can't wait to see you again in glory.*

*-KH*

---

For everything that was written in the past was written to teach us, so that through the endurance taught in the Scriptures and the encouragement they provide we might have hope.

ROMANS 15:4

# INTRODUCTION

After Jesus rose from the dead, he appeared to two of his followers on the road to Emmaus. "Beginning with Moses and all the Prophets, he explained to them what was said in all the Scriptures concerning himself" (Luke 24:27). Wouldn't you love to have been there? Can you imagine Jesus himself explaining the Scriptures, or can you guess which stories he shared? The Bible is filled with stories and pictures that point us to Jesus as the Savior, the One who can bring us back to God.

God had this plan for salvation way back in the beginning—before baby Jesus in the manger, before all those famous prophets and kings, before greats like Moses and Abraham, before Adam and Eve and their disobedience, and before the creation of people and bugs and trees and the entire world! Before it all, God had a plan to save his people—before he even created them (Ephesians 1:4; 1 Peter 1:18–20)! Jesus was not God's "Plan B" after Adam and Eve ate the forbidden fruit. The events of the Easter story were God's great plan all along!

God has the best plan, and the biggest and best story. As we dig into his salvation story over the next forty days, we are going to keep one important question at the forefront of our minds:

*Who is Jesus?*

Let's get started!

# HOW TO USE THIS BOOK

Each devotional includes a key verse, Bible passages for reference, and reflection questions. Choose whatever features are best for the various ages and attention spans in your family. Possible answers to most questions are included at the back of the book.

If your family enjoys singing as part of your devotional time, take note of the song suggestions in the back of the book corresponding to each day. Consider adding new songs your family enjoys so you can refer back to it year after year.

## HOW TO USE THIS BOOK FOR LENT AND EASTER

With forty days of readings, *Who Is Jesus?* fits perfectly as a family devotional leading up to Easter. If you'd like to follow the Lenten calendar, it begins on Ash Wednesday, six and a half weeks before Easter. (Lent traditionally does not include Sundays, including Easter Sunday.) If you get behind, don't worry! Day 35 is the Good Friday story, and Day 36 is the Easter story, so being a bit behind isn't necessarily a bad thing. You may also consider lighting candles to make your devotional time special.

# JESUS IS THE FIRSTBORN OVER ALL CREATION

The Son is the image of the invisible God, the firstborn over all creation.
For in him all things were created: things in heaven and on earth, visible and invisible,
whether thrones or powers or rulers or authorities; all things have been created
through him and for him. He is before all things, and in him all things hold together.

COLOSSIANS 1:15-17

In the beginning there was only God— God the Father, God the Son, and God the Holy Spirit. It was just the Trinity, together. There were no humans, no animals, no plants . . . nothing. Not even dirt! Genesis tells us "the earth was formless and empty, darkness was over the surface of the deep, and the Spirit of God was hovering over the waters" (1:2).

It was just God in the beginning—just God and an amazing plan. This plan involved his Son Jesus, and it also involves YOU.

God's masterful plan was bigger and better than anything you or I could ever dream up! God would make one special planet in the midst of a vast universe reaching farther than any human mind could comprehend. This planet, named Earth, would be a place where green things would grow, and where millions of intricately designed creatures would live. Bugs would crawl on delicate flowers, deer would dance through glowing meadows, and fish would dive in bubbling streams. God would take the empty, formless earth and make it full—full of life, color, noise, and beauty.

And then God would form human beings, special creatures made in his own likeness, in his image. These people would have the ability to know him well. They would walk and talk with him in a majestic garden. They would also be able to make choices, and sadly they would fail to make the right ones. Their disobedience and sin would separate them from God. Would it be sad? Yes. Would it be a surprise to God, proof that his plan had failed? No!

You see, in the beginning God had a plan—a plan to send his one and only Son, Jesus, to save the world by dying on a cross. God knew people would disobey him even before he created the first man Adam, but he created them anyway!

So God spoke.

He spoke and by the power of his voice he lovingly created our world. Out of the dust of the ground and the breath of his mouth, the first man, Adam, came into being, and from that man's rib came the first woman, Eve. God blessed them and commanded them to be fruitful, filling the earth with people who would rule over it and take care of it. God's wonderful plan was just beginning.

In the book of Colossians Paul gives Jesus, the center of God's plan, an important name: the firstborn over all creation (1:15). This doesn't mean that he was born first, or created first. Jesus existed before creation, and in fact *is* the Creator! To say that Jesus is the firstborn over all creation is to say that Jesus is exalted over all creation. The next verses tell us that all things are created by him and for him, and in him all things hold together. As Creator and Savior, he's the center and the focus. He's the most important, the most special, the most powerful. All creation glorifies *him*, the Savior, and he rules over it all forever.

# REFLECT

1. Which persons of the Trinity were present at creation?
See Genesis 1:2, 26; John 1:1–3; Colossians 1:15–17; and Revelation 13:8.

2. Can you name what God created on each day of creation?

3. What does it mean to be created in God's image?

4. How does it make you feel to know that God created
people even though he knew they would disobey him?

5. What does it mean that Jesus is the "firstborn over all creation"?

---

BIBLE REFERENCE GENESIS 1; JOHN 1:1-3

KEY VERSE COLOSSIANS 1:15-17

# JESUS IS
# THE SERPENT
# CRUSHER

---

"I will put enmity between you and the woman, between your offspring
and hers; he will crush your head, and you will strike his heel."

GENESIS 3:15

od made a home for Adam and Eve in the garden of Eden, a slice of heaven on earth. God assigned Adam to work in the garden and take care of it. Everything was perfect. Adam and Eve could eat from the Tree of Life and walk in the garden with God himself.

God gave them just one rule: they could not eat from the Tree of the Knowledge of Good and Evil. God warned Adam that if he ate of it, he would surely die.

Along came a crafty serpent, the devil himself. He tempted Eve to eat the fruit, telling her that when she ate it, she would be like God, knowing good and evil. Did Adam and Eve trust God, or would they eat the fruit?

The fruit looked so good! So Eve took a bite. Then she gave some to Adam, and he ate it too.

The world changed at that very moment. Adam and Eve had sinned. Their eyes were opened, and they realized they were naked. They sewed some fig leaves together to make clothes for themselves. And they hid from God.

"Where are you?" God called. He knew where they were. Perhaps he was fishing for a confession, or maybe he was asking, "Where are your hearts? Why didn't you trust me?"

Then it all spilled out. Adam and Eve started pointing fingers. Adam blamed Eve, and Eve blamed the serpent.

God is holy and just, and so are his actions. In response to their sin he brought pain, hard work, thorns, thistles, sweat, and dust. Dust—did you catch that? Adam would return to dust. In other words, he would die. Lastly, God banished them from the garden. No longer would they be able to eat from the Tree of Life. It's a sad, sad story.

But that's not the end of the story! God didn't just give out punishments; he also gave a promise. Because remember, God had a plan. Sin and evil would not win.

The promise came as God cursed the serpent, and it's easy to miss if we read too fast. God told the serpent, "I will put enmity between you and the woman, between your offspring and hers; he will crush your head, and you will strike his heel" (Genesis 3:15).

One day, one of Eve's descendants would defeat the serpent by crushing his head.

Who is this descendant, this serpent crusher? It's Jesus! Yes, the serpent would strike and Jesus would suffer, but Jesus would win!

How would this all happen? God gave us a clue when he made clothes for Adam and Eve out of animal skins. This was a beautiful gift, and not just because they wouldn't have to wear fig leaves anymore. God sacrificed an animal, one he had not long ago lovingly created, and used it to cover their bodies and the shame they now felt as a result of disobeying God. One day his Son Jesus would be sacrificed, erasing our sin and covering our shame, clothing us in righteousness instead. But the serpent would not win, because Jesus's death would not be the end of the story! Three days later Jesus would rise so that sin—and even death itself—would be crushed in Jesus's victory.

# REFLECT

1. How did sin enter the world? See Romans 5:12.

2. Why is sin such a big problem? See
Isaiah 59:2 and Romans 3:23; 6:23.

3. Where do we see the promise of Jesus
in this story? See Genesis 3:15.

———————————

**BIBLE REFERENCE** GENESIS 3

**KEY VERSE** GENESIS 3:15

# JESUS IS THE ARK AND THE DOOR

"I am the door.
If anyone enters by me,
he will be saved."

JOHN 10:9A ESV

oah's ark sounds like just about the cutest story in the Bible, doesn't it? You've probably seen pictures of wide-eyed baby tigers scampering next to bunnies, mice riding on the backs of elephants, and giraffes so tall their poor skinny necks have to stick out the windows.

But all those cute illustrations can give us the wrong idea of the story. It's kind of a scary one, actually. It's about God's hatred of sin and his judgment because of it. You see, in Noah's time, people were very wicked. It was so bad that the Bible says every thought in their hearts was evil all the time (Genesis 6:5). The Bible says God was grieved that he had made people and his heart was filled with pain (6:6). So he decided to send the flood.

Noah wasn't perfect; he was born into sin just like you and me. But the Bible tells us he was a righteous man who walked with God. And he had great faith. We know this because when God told him to build a giant boat in a place with likely very little water, he obeyed, down to the smallest detail. His neighbors probably thought he was crazy!

When Noah finished the boat, he, his family, and the animals entered the ark. Then God shut the door. Not long after that, the rains God had promised started to pour.

The rains came down and the fountains of the deep opened up. Rain, rain, and more rain for forty days; more than you can possibly imagine! Rain of judgment over sin, and perhaps the tears of God. The water covered the mountains, so all living things on the ground died. Only Noah, his family, and the animals on board survived.

After the waters finally receded, God told Noah to leave the ark with his family and all the animals. What joy they must have felt walking through the door and onto dry ground at last! Noah built an altar and burned an offering to thank and praise God. The Lord smelled the soothing aroma of the offering and was pleased. Then he made a covenant with Noah, a promise to never flood the entire earth again. He gave the rainbow as a sign of his promise and his great mercy.

Did the flood fix the problem of sin? No, people still sinned. Even Noah, the man who "walked" with God, sinned after the flood. God's plan was that Jesus would be the ark that we can enter into and be saved. Jesus is our ark and he's the one and only door to salvation (John 10:9). Just as God was pleased with Noah's sacrifice after the flood, one day he would be pleased with another, far greater sacrifice, the sacrifice of his Son Jesus.

God has provided a way for us to escape the floodwaters of sin. Will you trust God as Noah did? Will you enter into the perfect ark?

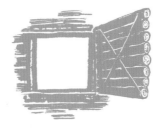

# REFLECT

1. How is Jesus like our ark?

2. Read John 10:9 and discuss how it relates to our story today. Note that some versions use "gate" and others use "door."

3. Read Genesis 9:12–16 ESV, and think about not just a rainbow, but a hunting bow. What do you think God is saying here?

4. Read Revelation 4:3 and discuss why we might be seeing a rainbow here.

5. Read Genesis 8:20–22. What comfort does this bring to you?

---

BIBLE REFERENCE GENESIS 6:1–9:17

KEY VERSE JOHN 10:9A ESV

# JESUS IS THE ONE THROUGH WHOM THE WORLD IS BLESSED

---

*"All peoples on earth will be blessed through you."*

GENESIS 12:3B

eet Abram, a man whose remarkable faith gives him the most verses in Hebrews 11's "hall of fame." A man who, unlike many familiar Bible figures, didn't grow up knowing God, but instead his family worshiped idols. Then God spoke to him, asking him to leave his home and go to the land God would show him.

God said, "I will make you into a great nation, and I will bless you; I will make your name great and you will be a blessing. I will bless those who bless you, and whoever curses you I will curse; and all peoples on earth will be blessed through you" (Genesis 12:2–3).

Abram trusted this God he barely knew and embarked on an incredible journey into the unknown. He left behind his home of many years and all that was familiar. But many years passed, and he and his wife Sarai still had no children. How would he become a great nation?

Then God came to Abram again. "Do not be afraid, Abram, I am your shield, your very great reward" (Genesis 15:1).

God invited Abram to look up at the clear night sky. Could he count the stars? That's how many descendants he would have! Abram looked and he believed God's promise. And the Lord credited it to him as righteousness (15:6).

Then something strange happened. Well, it seems strange to us, but it wasn't to Abram. You see, in Abram's time people would make promises to each other by cutting up animals, and then walking between them. It seems kind of gross, but in effect what they were saying was, "If I break my promise, let me be like this animal!" This was serious business! Both people making the covenant would have to walk through, both promising the other could take their life if they didn't keep their side of the covenant.

God told Abram to bring him a heifer, a goat, and a ram, each three years old, along with a dove and a young pigeon. Abram brought them and knew what to do. He cut them in two and arranged them with the halves opposite each other.

The sun began to set, and Abram fell into a deep sleep. The Bible says that a thick and dreadful darkness came over him, which means he was really scared! God told Abram about his future, and the future of his descendants. Then a smoking firepot and a blazing torch appeared, both symbolizing the presence of God, and they passed between the bloody pieces. Abram didn't have to walk through—just God! God took all the responsibility of keeping the covenant. What relief Abram must have felt!

More years passed, and when Abram was 100 years old, he did have a son and then eventually many descendants. But one of these descendants would truly make Abram the father of many. His name was Jesus, and through his death and resurrection, all who believe are welcomed into Abraham's family and can share in the blessing.

If you are a child of God, you are a child of Abraham. One of those stars was lit for you! You are loved and pursued as Abraham was. You are forgiven and righteous. You will have blessing and great inheritance. You are blessed to be a blessing. And God, the covenant keeper, assures all these blessings through the blood of his Son Jesus. Like Abraham, we could never keep the covenant on our own, so the Son of God gives his own life, and we must believe.

Jesus said, "For God so loved the world, that he gave his only Son, that whoever believes in him should not perish but have eternal life" (John 3:16). What a blessing!

# REFLECT

1. Did you notice that Abram's name changed to Abraham?
God did this! Do you know what each name means?

2. Read Genesis 15:6 and try to explain it in your own words.

3. Why is it significant that only God passed through the dead animals, not Abram?

4. How have you been blessed, and how can you be a blessing to others?

---

**BIBLE REFERENCE** GENESIS 12:1-3; 15:1-21;
GALATIANS 3:6-9; HEBREWS 11:8-12

**KEY VERSE** GENESIS 12:3

# JESUS IS THE LAMB GOD HAS PROVIDED

---

*"Look, the Lamb of God, who takes away the sin of the world!"*

JOHN 1:29B

or years, Abraham and Sarah waited, prayed, and hoped. At last, God blessed them with a son. They named him Isaac, which means "he laughs." Oh, the laughter! First laughter of disbelief that such an old man and old woman could have a son, but then laughter of joy and thanksgiving! Isaac was the son of the promise, the son who would make Abraham the father of many nations. Finally God's promises seemed to be setting into motion. Abraham probably gazed at the stars every night and thought about his future grandchildren and the blessings they were promised.

Then God did something surprising: he tested Abraham.

"Abraham!" God spoke.

"Here I am," Abraham replied.

"Take your son, your only son, whom you love—Isaac—and go to the region of Moriah. Sacrifice him there as a burnt offering on one of the mountains I will show you" (Genesis 22:2).

Now Abraham had built many altars and burned many sacrifices to worship God. But sacrifice his son? His only son? The son of the promise?

It must have seemed unthinkable, but Abraham reasoned that if Isaac did die, God could raise him from the dead (Hebrews 11:19). Talk about incredible faith!

The next morning Abraham got up early and obediently headed out on a three-day journey to the mountain with his dear son Isaac. When they reached Moriah, he told his servants to stay with the donkey while he and Isaac went up to worship, saying they would be back.

Abraham put the wood on Isaac's back and they started climbing.

"Father," Isaac asked, "where is the lamb for a burnt offering?"

"God himself will provide the lamb for the burnt offering, my son" (Genesis 22:8).

They continued on until they reached the place God had told him about. Abraham built an altar and arranged the wood. Still no lamb.

Then Abraham bound Isaac and laid him on the altar. Isaac, being much younger and stronger than his father, probably could have resisted him, but that's not what we see in the Bible. Instead, he obediently submitted to his father's will.

Abraham took the knife and raised it to slay his son.

"Abraham! Abraham!" the angel of the Lord called out. "Do not lay a hand on the boy! Do not do anything to him. Now I know that you fear God, because you have not withheld from me your son, your only son" (22:12).

What relief they must have felt! And nearby there was a ram, caught by its horns in the thicket. A substitute—a merciful substitute! Abraham grabbed the ram and sacrificed it on the altar instead of his son. Then Abraham named the place "The Lord Will Provide."

The Lord had provided a ram to sacrifice instead of Isaac. Isaac could live.

Many years later God's Son, his only Son, would carry the wood of the cross on his back—the cross that would become a place of sacrifice. He would do it willingly, as Isaac did. Only God would not spare him as he spared Isaac. There would be no ram in the thicket, no other way to atone but through the flesh of God himself. Jesus is the lamb that Abraham believed God would provide, the Lamb of God who takes away the sin of the world.

# REFLECT

1. How many similarities can you find between the story of
Abraham and Isaac and the death of Jesus?

2. What is one major difference between the story of Abraham and Isaac
and the death of Jesus? See Matthew 26:53 and Romans 8:32.

3. Read John 1:29. What do you think the people of
Jesus's day thought when they heard this?

4. What did Abraham name the mountain, and what
was/is the significance of that name?

---

**BIBLE REFERENCE** GENESIS 22:1-19; HEBREWS 11:17-19

**KEY VERSE** JOHN 1:29B

# JESUS IS THE STAIRWAY TO HEAVEN

"Very truly I tell you, you will see 'heaven open, and the angels of God ascending and descending on' the Son of Man."

JOHN 1:51

acob was on the run. Before he and his twin brother were born, God told their mother that they would fight with each other. Esau would be born first, but Jacob would come out ahead in the end. He would be the blessed one, and his older brother would serve him.

Jacob—the liar, the trickster—was the son God had chosen to inherit the blessing promised to Abraham and Isaac, the one to bring his blessing to the world. God was going to grab hold of him and make him into a great nation. God loves to take our hard and deceitful hearts and melt them to use them for his glory.

Jacob had done something so deceitful that his brother Esau wanted to kill him. He had taken Esau's birthright and blessing right out from under his nose. Esau wanted revenge, and so Jacob fled.

When Jacob stopped for the night with only a stone for a pillow, he went to sleep and had a dream. He saw a giant staircase, starting on the ground and reaching all the way up to heaven. Angels were going up and down the steps. And then way up at the very top of the stairway was the Lord himself.

The Lord spoke: "I am the LORD, the God of your father Abraham and the God of Isaac. I will give you and your descendants the land on which you are lying. Your descendants will be like the dust of the earth, and you will spread out to the west and to the east, to the north and to the south. All peoples on earth will be blessed through you and your offspring" (Genesis 28:13–14).

Jacob knew these promises! These were the same promises given to his grandfather Abraham! And then God added more—promises that meant a great deal to a runaway heavy with guilt.

"I am with you and will watch over you wherever you go, and I will bring you back to this land. I will not leave you until I have done what I have promised you" (Genesis 28:15).

Then Jacob woke up. God's presence had been there! God himself had spoken to him! Had he found the house of God, the gate of heaven itself? What an awesome place he was standing on! He knew he was going to be okay. God would be with him. God had promised his blessing.

Jacob looked at the stone he had used to rest his head. He set it up as a pillar, a standing stone, a way to remember this place. Then he poured oil on it and called the place Bethel, which means "House of God."

Jacob made a vow that day that God would be his God, and he promised to give a tenth of all he had to him. Then he continued on his journey, trusting God to guide his steps.

Is there really a stairway to heaven, one we could walk up and see God himself? Jesus gives us the answer in the book of John. He said, "Very truly I tell you, you will see 'heaven open, and the angels of God ascending and descending on' the Son of Man" (John 1:51). Jesus is telling us that he is the stairway. We can't get to God without him! "I am the way and the truth and the life. No one comes to the Father except through me" (John 14:6).

# REFLECT

1. How many ways are there to get to heaven?

2. How is Jesus like a stairway to heaven?

3. How do you think you would have reacted to the dream if you were Jacob?

4. Why do you think God chose to reveal himself to Jacob when Jacob was such a trickster? What comfort can this bring to us?

---

**BIBLE REFERENCE** GENESIS 28:10-22

**KEY VERSE** JOHN 1:51

## DAY
## 7

# JESUS IS
# THE BETRAYED AND
# THE SAVIOR

And we have seen and testify that the Father has sent his Son to be the Savior of the world.

1 JOHN 4:14

he last major story in the book of Genesis is the incredible true tale of Joseph the dreamer. Throughout the story, God weaves glimpses of Jesus and of his master plan of redemption.

Jacob had twelve sons, but Joseph was his favorite. Jacob gave Joseph a richly ornamented robe to show his love for him. This special treatment made his brothers so mad that they hated him. If that wasn't enough, Joseph had dreams that his brothers' sheaves of grain were bowing down to his sheaf of grain, and that the sun and moon and eleven stars were bowing

down to him. His brothers were outraged. "Will we bow down to you? Surely not!"

They had to get rid of him. If they killed him, they would smother his dreams as well!

One day in a faraway field, Joseph's brothers attacked him and threw him in an empty cistern. A caravan came by, and Joseph's brother Judah came up with a plan. "What will we gain if we kill him? Let's sell him instead!" So they pulled Joseph out and sold him for twenty pieces of silver. The brothers killed a goat and dipped Joseph's fancy robe in it. They brought the robe to their father and told him Joseph was killed by a wild animal.

God was with Joseph. He was sold to Potiphar, an Egyptian official. The Lord gave Joseph success in everything he did (Genesis 39:3) and he was very well respected. Things didn't go well forever, though. Potiphar's wife accused Joseph of doing something he didn't do, and Joseph landed in jail. Figuratively speaking, he was thrown into a pit all over again!

Was God still with Joseph? Absolutely yes. God made Joseph the dreamer into the dream interpreter, and he ended up interpreting a dream for Pharaoh, the Egyptian king! The dream revealed that there would be seven years of plenty in Egypt, and then seven years of famine. Joseph suggested that Pharaoh appoint someone to be in charge of saving food during the years of plenty so the nation would survive the years of famine. And who do you think Pharaoh appointed? Joseph, of course! The prison was no longer his home; he moved to the palace!

Pharaoh's dream came true; and after that, Joseph's dreams came true as well. You see, back home his family was starving from the famine. So Joseph's father, Jacob, sent his sons to buy grain in Egypt. When they arrived, they bowed down before their brother, begging for grain. It was just like his dream!

Joseph didn't reveal himself right away, but when he did, he showed complete forgiveness, weeping and hugging them. He knew wholeheartedly that God had sent him to Egypt to save many lives, including the lives of his brothers, God's chosen people. He said, "You intended to harm me, but God intended it for good" (Genesis 50:20).

Joseph was his family's savior from a famine, but he points us to Jesus, the Savior from sin. Like Joseph, Jesus would have to leave his home and his father. His own brothers would think he was out of his mind, not believing his words. People would hate him so much that they would want him dead, and he would be betrayed and sold out for silver coins. He would be punished even though he was innocent. And as sad as all of that sounds, it would all be part of a master plan! God would use all of the terrible things that happened to his Son Jesus for good. For our good! For the saving of many lives (Genesis 50:20)!

You see, when God has a saving plan for his people, a pit and a prison aren't going to stop him—not even the pit of death itself. God will save his people and bring about good, because God is good!

Joseph was a temporary savior, but you can be sure that Jesus is our true Savior. The grain God's people received in this story gave them the bread their bellies grumbled for—the bread they needed to physically survive. But their hearts would still hunger for more, and Jesus would be the answer.

# REFLECT

1. What are the similarities between Joseph's story and Jesus's story?

2. Can you give an example from your own life of something that started out as a bad situation but God used it for good?

3. Read Genesis 44:33, where Judah offers his life in place of Benjamin's. How might this section of the story point us to Jesus?

---

**BIBLE REFERENCE** GENESIS 37; 39–45

**KEY VERSE** 1 JOHN 4:14

# DAY 8

# JESUS IS THE DELIVERER

"The Spirit of the Lord is on me, because he has anointed me
to proclaim good news to the poor. He has sent me to proclaim
freedom for the prisoners and recovery of sight for the blind, to set
the oppressed free, to proclaim the year of the Lord's favor."

LUKE 4:18-19

Joseph's family stayed in Egypt hundreds of years, and during that time their family grew, and grew, and grew, just as God had promised. A time came, though, when the Egyptians saw the growing group of Israelites and got nervous. *They are getting too numerous! Too powerful! What if they revolt?* And so the Egyptians forced the Israelites into slavery.

Once again God's people needed saving, and they cried out to him. God heard their cries and sent them Moses, a man with a pretty unique past.

You see, Moses was born an Israelite but was raised as an Egyptian. How did this happen?

Sadly, there's more to the story. Pharaoh decided to stop the Israelites from gaining too much power by killing all the baby boys. "Throw them in the Nile River!" he said.

It was right at this time that Moses was born. His parents saw that he was no ordinary child, and they were not afraid of the king's edict, so they hid him for three months (Hebrews 11:23). When they could hide him no longer, his mother made a basket of papyrus, coating it with tar and pitch, fashioning it into a miniature ark for her son, and placing it in the river.

When Pharaoh's daughter went down to the river to bathe, she found the baby, and she felt sorry for him. God used Pharaoh's own daughter to rescue the one who would rescue his people. So Moses grew up in the palace, as a son of royalty.

One day when he was grown up, he saw an Egyptian beating one of his own people. In anger he killed the Egyptian. Now he was in trouble! He fled Egypt and moved to the dry and desolate land of Midian.

It was there in the desert that God spoke to Moses. Oh, how often God speaks to us in desert places! God came to Moses in the form of fire, in a bush that burned without burning up. This was the first of many times Moses would see God in the form of fire—his burning presence, wonderful, scary, holy, overwhelming, and awesome.

"Moses! Moses! . . . I have indeed seen the misery of my people in Egypt. I have heard them crying out because of their slave drivers, and I am concerned about their suffering. So I have come down to rescue them from the hand of the Egyptians and to bring them up out of that land into a good and spacious land, a land flowing with milk and honey. . . . So now, go. I am sending you to Pharaoh to bring my people the Israelites out of Egypt" (Exodus 3:4b, 7–8, 10).

Moses was scared. But little did he know how God had been equipping him. God always has a plan. Moses was equipped to talk to Pharaoh, having grown up in his house. He was equipped to lead God's people into the desert, a foreign place for them, because he had spent years as a shepherd in the desert of Midian. He would shepherd those people, much like he had shepherded sheep. Despite Moses's fear and reluctance, God would use him in marvelous ways.

Years later, another terrible king, King Herod, would make a law that all the baby boys who threatened his power be killed. Two young parents, Joseph and Mary, would take their son Jesus and flee to the land of Egypt. They would live there until God called them out again, just as he did with the children of Israel.

Jesus would become the deliverer, just as Moses was—a prince stepping down to save his dearly loved people. Just as God came down into the burning bush to rescue his people from slavery in Egypt, his Son Jesus would come down to rescue the world from their slavery to sin. He would be like Moses the deliverer, only so much greater. He would lead them not just to the promised land of Canaan, but to the promised kingdom of heaven, to forever freedom.

# REFLECT

1. How does Moses point us to Jesus?

2. What do we need to be delivered from?
See Hosea 13:14; Matthew 6:13; Galatians 1:4.

3. How many times do you think the story of the Israelites' deliverance from Egypt is mentioned in the Bible? Why so often? See Exodus 20:2 and Deuteronomy 4:37 for examples.

4. Moses was not perfect, as Jesus was, and yet God used him. How might God be preparing you for service in his kingdom, or how might he want to use you today?

---

**BIBLE REFERENCE** EXODUS 1–4; MATTHEW 2:13–16

**KEY VERSE** LUKE 4:18–19

# JESUS IS THE PASSOVER LAMB

---

For Christ, our Passover lamb, has been sacrificed.

1 CORINTHIANS 5:7B

oses was God's chosen leader, the deliverer, equipped for the task and empowered by God. In spite of his reluctance and fear, Moses obeyed God and approached Pharaoh, saying, "Let my people go!"

But Pharaoh's heart was hard, and he refused. So God sent miraculous signs and wonders. He first turned the Nile River to blood. The Nile supplied the Egyptians' drinking water, their transportation, their fertile soil, their papyrus for making paper, and more. It was what made them prosperous and wealthy—it was their source of life! And God turned it into a bloody river of death.

But was that enough to make Pharaoh relent? No. So God sent more plagues. Plagues of frogs, gnats, flies, dying animals, boils, hail, and locusts. God was showing his power over the gods of the Egyptians. No amount of praying to the river god, the sky god, the agriculture god, the cattle god, the skin diseases god, or any other god would help them, because those gods weren't real!

But still Pharaoh would not let the Israelites go.

After eight terrible plagues, God sent the plague of darkness. To us it doesn't seem worse than frogs in your bed, or all your food for the next year being eaten up by locusts, but to the Egyptians it was a big deal. You see, the Egyptians' most important god was Re, the sun god, and the pharaoh himself was considered a son of Re. Through this plague God was telling the Egyptians, "Your gods aren't real! Re isn't helping you, is he? I'm more powerful than even the sun itself!"

But that was not the worst. The tenth plague would be the one that would push Pharaoh over the edge. It would be so awful that Pharaoh would beg that they leave, sending them with plunder of gold, silver, and clothes. The tenth plague would be the Israelites' ticket to freedom, a night they would remember forever.

Moses warned Pharaoh, but still he would not listen. At midnight God would travel through the land of Egypt, killing the firstborn son in every house. But the Israelite homes would be spared if they followed the Lord's instructions.

Each family was to choose a perfect year-old lamb and slaughter it. Then they must take some of its blood and put it on the sides and tops of the doorframes of their houses. That night they must eat the meat of the lamb, roasted over the fire, along with bitter herbs and bread made without yeast. They must eat quickly and be ready to go; their cloak tucked into their belt, their sandals on their feet, and their staff in hand.

With the sign of blood on the doorframes of their homes, the Lord would pass over them, not letting the angel of death enter.

That night would become known as the Passover, because God literally passed over the homes of the Israelites, but in every Egyptian house someone was dead. God spared his people because he saw the blood of the lamb. For generations they would celebrate this night, sacrificing a lamb and telling their children how God had delivered them from slavery.

This Passover and all those sacrificed lambs point us to another act of mercy and one perfect Lamb. Jesus became the final, perfect Lamb, slain for our sake. When God sees the blood of his Son marking the doorframes of our hearts, his judgment passes over us. He spares us from his wrath, and instead welcomes us to his promised land.

# REFLECT

1. Do some research as a family on the gods of the Egyptians. What gods might each plague be attacking?

2. How was Jesus the perfect Lamb? See 1 Peter 1:19.

3. Why is this night called the Passover?

4. Jesus celebrated the Passover with his disciples. Read Matthew 26:26–29. What reason did Jesus give for pouring out his blood?

---

**BIBLE REFERENCE** EXODUS 4–12

**KEY VERSE** 1 CORINTHIANS 5:7B

# JESUS IS
# THE ROCK
# MOSES STRUCK

---

*For they drank from the spiritual rock that accompanied
them, and that rock was Christ.*

1 CORINTHIANS 10:4

he Israelites left Egypt, finally free from 430 years of slavery! God was with them, leading them with a pillar of cloud in the day and a pillar of fire at night. But when Pharaoh changed his mind and began to chase after the Israelites, the people panicked. They were trapped between an army and a huge sea. Immediately they blamed Moses for bringing them out of Egypt and said they wished he would have left them alone! How quickly they forgot all the signs and wonders of God in Egypt and how he spared them in the Passover!

"Do not be afraid," Moses said. "Stand firm and you will see the deliverance the LORD will bring you today. The Egyptians you see today you will never see again. The LORD will fight for you; you need only to be still" (Exodus 14:13–14).

God told Moses to raise his staff and stretch his hand over the sea. Moses obeyed, and God drove the water back with a strong wind, creating a dry path for the people to walk on. The angel of the Lord and the pillar of cloud went behind them, blocking the Egyptian army. All the Israelites, walking between walls of water on each side, made it safely across, but when the Egyptians followed, the Lord looked down from the cloud and fire and sent the army into confusion, making their chariot wheels fall off. Then God told Moses to stretch out his hand again, and the waters crashed on the Egyptians, drowning the whole army.

The Israelites, seeing God's power once again, feared the Lord and put their trust in him.

But after three days of traveling, they began to grumble again against Moses. They were thirsty, and the only water they had was bitter. God showed Moses a piece of wood, and Moses threw it in the water, making it sweet.

They drank the water, but the sweetness of it didn't change their bitter attitudes, and soon they were grumbling again. They were hungry! So God rained down bread from heaven to feed his people.

Again the Israelites traveled, and again they had no water. Did they remember how God took care of them before with miraculous signs and wonders? Did they remember how the Lord fought for them? Did they trust God to take care of their daily needs?

No, instead they put God to the test. They grumbled against Moses. "Why did you bring us up out of Egypt to make us and our children and livestock die of thirst?" (Exodus 17:3b).

Moses cried out to the Lord, "What am I to do with these people? They are almost ready to stone me" (17:4).

God could have punished his people in anger. They were failing the test! They weren't trusting him! In fact, they were testing him instead, saying, "Is the LORD among us or not?" (17:7).

But God, in grace and compassion, gave them the water they asked for, and a hint of something more.

God told Moses to take his staff—the staff he had used to strike the Nile, turning it to blood, and the staff that was raised over the sea that drowned the Egyptians—a staff used for judgment.

And God said he would stand before Moses on a rock. Then God told him to strike the rock, and water would come out of it for the people to drink.

Moses obeyed, and it happened just as God said it would. Moses named that place Massah and Meribah, meaning "testing" and "rebellion."

Do you see what God did here? Instead of striking the people for their rebellion, God wanted the rock that *he* was standing on to be struck instead. In 1 Corinthians 10:4, Paul tells us that Jesus Christ is that rock. The people deserved the judgment, but Jesus took it. And from that rock flowed water to quench their thirst. That moment pointed to the day when Jesus's side would be struck, and water would flow from him—water and blood that give us life.

Is the Lord among us or not? He is! And he is full of grace, having already taken our judgment upon himself.

# REFLECT

1. How do we see God fighting for his people in this story?

2. Read John 19:33–37 and Isaiah 53:4–6. How do these passages relate to today's story?

3. How does God ask you to trust him on a daily basis?

4. In what ways do you see that the Lord is among us today?

---

BIBLE REFERENCE EXODUS 17:1–7

KEY VERSE 1 CORINTHIANS 10:4

# JESUS IS THE MEDIATOR

For this reason Christ is the mediator of a new covenant, that those who are called may receive the promised eternal inheritance—now that he has died as a ransom to set them free from the sins committed under the first covenant.

HEBREWS 9:15

od led his people to the base of Mount Sinai. They would spend a year in this place, learning all sorts of rules for how they were to obey God and worship him.

But really it wasn't just about the rules. It was about much more. God spoke to the people through Moses, inviting them into a covenant with him. It was something like a contract, with duties on both sides—and something like a marriage, where the husband loves and cares for his wife, and the wife loves him back and serves as his helper. God reminded his people that he was their deliverer, the one who carried them out of Egypt on eagles' wings. He wanted to enter into a covenant with them, a covenant in which they would obey him fully, and in return they would be his treasured possession. And they would have an important mission. They would become a kingdom of priests, a holy nation. A nation on display to the world, showing all people who the God of the universe is, and what he is like. A nation who by their example would bring glory to God, and bring others into relationship with him.

The people all responded to God's covenant by saying,

"We will do everything the LORD has said" (Exodus 19:8). And God responded with his Presence in a dense cloud, and with thunder, lightning, trumpet blasts, fire, and smoke. The whole mountain shook, and the people trembled with fear. They begged Moses to speak to them instead of hearing directly from God, for they were afraid they would die.

Moses approached the thick darkness where God was, and God spoke to him. God gave him many laws for holy living, including the Ten Commandments, which showed the people how to love God and how to love others.

Moses was gone for forty days on the mountain. The people began to get anxious, and they demanded that Moses's brother, Aaron, help them make gods to lead them. Imagine that! How quickly they gave up on Moses, and on God, who only days before had entered into a special covenant with them! Aaron foolishly helped the people make a calf out of gold, and they worshiped it, saying, "This is the god who brought us out of Egypt" (Exodus 32:4, paraphrase)!

How do you think God responded? He was angry, of course! These people, whom he had made his treasured possession, had turned their backs on him already! God's anger burned against them, and he wanted to destroy them.

But Moses spoke up for the people, pleading for them. He boldly challenged God to think of what the Egyptians would say. He reminded God of his covenant with Abraham, Isaac, and Jacob. He begged God to turn from his anger and relent. And God did.

In his mercy, God remembered his covenant. He promised to lead his people to the promised land. But this time he said his Presence would not go with them.

Again, Moses pleaded with God. He knew they needed his Presence! He said, "How will anyone know that you are pleased with me and with your people unless you go with us? What else will distinguish me and your people from all the other people on the face of the earth?" (Exodus 33:16).

God listened, and promised to do the very thing Moses asked. His Presence would go with them.

Moses took it one step further. "Now show me your glory," he said (33:18). God directed Moses to a cleft of a rock. God passed by, allowing Moses to see his back, but not his face. When Moses came down the mountain, his face glowed with the glory of God.

Moses continued to serve as a mediator for God's people. He was the go-between, the man in the middle, the messenger, and the pleader for reconciliation. Moses is long gone, but today we have another mediator—a mediator with whom God is pleased, just as he was with Moses. A mediator who goes between us and God, pleading for us. A mediator who ascended a hill to make atonement for sin. But he's greater than Moses, because he's perfect, makes complete atonement, and is God himself. This mediator is Jesus! And today, because of him, we can be reconciled to God and enjoy his Presence.

# REFLECT

1. What did Moses do for the people as mediator?

2. How is Jesus our mediator? See Hebrews 9:15 and 1 John 2:1-2.

3. Why do we end our prayers with the words, "in Jesus's name, amen"?

---

**BIBLE REFERENCE** EXODUS 19:1-9; 32; 33:12-23

**KEY VERSE** HEBREWS 9:15

# JESUS IS THE TABERNACLE

---

The Word became flesh and made his dwelling among us.
We have seen his glory, the glory of the one and only Son,
who came from the Father, full of grace and truth.

JOHN 1:14

ack in the garden of Eden, Adam and Eve enjoyed a perfect relationship with their creator. Because they were sinless, they were able to enjoy God's Presence in a way that's hard to wrap our minds around. But now God's people were tainted with sin. How could a perfect God dwell among them? Moses knew the people needed God's Presence so much that he begged for it, and God knew it too. That's why he already had a plan in place. God wanted the people to make a sanctuary, a tabernacle, for him to dwell in. But it had to be a certain way. The book of Hebrews tells us that

Moses's tabernacle was a copy and shadow of what is in heaven, and it takes many, many chapters in Exodus for Moses to learn how to make it. This tent in the desert was really important!

The tabernacle had three major parts: the courtyard, the Holy Place, and the Most Holy Place. The courtyard was the area that was visible and accessible to most people. It had two important parts to it: the altar and the basin. The altar was very important, because it was how the people made sacrifices to the Lord—to thank him, to worship him, and to atone for their sins. Many animals were burned on this altar, including young bulls, goats, lambs, pigeons, and doves. Behind the altar was the bronze basin, where the priests would wash their hands and feet to cleanse themselves.

Beyond the altar and the basin was the tent itself. The first room inside the tent was the Holy Place. To the right was the table of the bread of the Presence, with twelve loaves of bread for the twelve tribes of Israel. To the left was the lampstand, beautifully hammered from one piece of gold in the shape of an almond tree, giving light to the room. At the far end was the altar of incense. It burned sweet-smelling spices, with smoke rising in front of the curtain, representing the prayers of God's people rising up to him.

The curtain itself was decorated with cherubim, and it shielded, or veiled, the priests from the next room, the Most Holy Place, or the Holy of Holies, where God's Presence was. This room was shaped like a cube, and the high priest was only allowed to enter the room once a year on the Day of Atonement. In this room there was only one thing: the ark of the covenant, also known as the ark of the testimony.

Imagine the people's excitement when the tabernacle was finished. They had been a part of it! They had brought their precious metals and stones. They had used their talents to sew priestly garments and hammer beautiful things from gold. They had watched as it all came together. And now God's Presence was going to come fill it as he had promised! A cloud settled on the tent, and the glory of the Lord filled the tabernacle. The cloud was over the tabernacle by day, and fire was in the cloud by night. When the cloud moved, the people would set out, so God's Presence would always be with them.

The book of John tells us that Jesus came to earth to dwell, or "tabernacle," among us (John 1:14). Much like the tabernacle of the Old Testament, Jesus would be God's Presence, living and moving among his people. He would be our access to God, our means of atonement, and our tangible, direct link to God. After all, he's God himself! Jesus explained this when he was in the temple (which had replaced the tabernacle). He said to the teachers, "Destroy this temple, and I will raise it again in three days" (John 2:19). In other words, he was saying, "I am the temple! I am God's Presence!" He knew they would kill him, but he also knew he would rise three days later. The precious pieces of the tabernacle and temple would no longer be needed to enjoy God's Presence or make atonement, because Jesus himself would be the meeting place between God and his people.

Today we not only have Jesus, but we also have the gift of the Holy Spirit that God sent at Pentecost. We can enjoy the Presence of God in our lives at all times thanks to what Jesus accomplished on the cross and in our hearts and lives. Thank God today for his Presence. We so desperately need it!

# REFLECT

1. How was God present with his people in the desert?

2. How is he present with us today?

3. What were the different pieces of the tabernacle, and what were they used for?

4. What happened to the curtain when Jesus died on the cross (Matthew 27:51)? What was the significance of this?

5. Revelation 21 tells us about the New Jerusalem. What is the shape of it (see verse 16)? Is there a tabernacle or temple? Why or why not (verse 22)?

---

**BIBLE REFERENCE** EXODUS 25:1-9; 40:34-38

**KEY VERSE** JOHN 1:14

# JESUS IS THE MERCY SEAT

God presented Christ as a sacrifice of atonement, through
the shedding of his blood—to be received by faith.

ROMANS 3:25A

e already learned about the tabernacle in the wilderness, the place of God's Presence among his people. Now let's close our eyes and take a walk. Enter the courtyard, go past the altar and the basin, and step into the Holy Place. Notice the bread on the table and the golden lampstand bringing light to the tent. See the smoke rising in front of the curtain decorated with angels. Carefully move aside the heavy curtain and step into the Most Holy Place. What do you see? Just one thing: the ark of the covenant, a beautiful chest covered with a lid of pure gold. Two golden angels sit on the lid, facing each other with their wings spread upward, covering the ark. What are they doing? Worshiping? Guarding? And what's in the box? I'll tell you. Inside the box are the stone tablets with the Ten Commandments, a jar of manna, and Aaron's budded staff. This chest with its lid, known as the atonement cover or mercy seat, is the most special part of the entire tabernacle. Why? Because it was right here, in this small but special place, that God's Presence came. Right on the cover between the cherubim (Exodus 25:22).

If this were Bible times, you would *not* be allowed in here! (You can open your eyes now.) This place was *very* special and *very* holy. *Only* the high priest could go behind the curtain into the Most Holy Place, and *only* on the Day of Atonement, which was *only* once a year! And even then he had to be sure to wash himself, wear his sacred garments, and follow very specific instructions for sacrifice. Even that was not enough. He also had to burn incense so that the smoke from it would hide the mercy seat and the glorious Presence of God from his sight, or he would die! This was a holy place!

So what was the high priest doing in there that was so important? Why would he even dare to go in there? He had a very, very important job to do. Something that was necessary for the Israelites to maintain their relationship with the one true Holy God. His job was to sprinkle the blood of a sacrificed goat on the mercy seat to atone for the sins of the people. Blood was what God required as payment for sins. This atonement cover, this mercy seat, drenched in blood, was the place where an unholy people were reconciled to a holy God.

In the book of Romans, Paul tells us that God presented Jesus as a sacrifice of atonement (Romans 3:25). The phrase "sacrifice of atonement" is the same Greek word that is translated as "mercy seat" in Hebrews 9:5.[1] Paul is telling us that Jesus is the mercy seat. Jesus is the "place" where we are reconciled to God. He is stained with blood for our sake. He is the atonement cover for our sin. We can join with the cherubim surrounding his throne of grace singing, "Worthy is the Lamb, who was slain" (Revelation 5:12)!

Today we don't have a tabernacle. We don't have a curtain separating us from God. We don't have to kill a goat to pay for our sins or rely on a priest to help us. We have Jesus living among us, the One who made atonement once for all. His body was torn just as the curtain was (Hebrews 10:20), so we don't have to be separated from God ever again. Jesus is the way we are able to meet with God. Thank you, God, for your mercy!

# REFLECT

1. Describe the ark and the mercy seat. What did
they look like? What was their purpose?

2. How is Jesus like the mercy seat?

3. Read John 20:11-13. What similarities can we draw between
the angels in this story and the cherubim on the ark?

4. Read Leviticus 16:20-22, about the Day of Atonement.
How is Jesus like the scapegoat?

---

BIBLE REFERENCE EXODUS 25:10-22;
LEVITICUS 16:1-19; HEBREWS 9:1-5

KEY VERSE ROMANS 3:25A

# JESUS IS THE
# ONE WHO
# IS LIFTED UP

---

*"Just as Moses lifted up the snake in the wilderness, so the Son of Man must
be lifted up, that everyone who believes may have eternal life in him."*

JOHN 3:14-15

**B**y now you know that the Israelites weren't perfect. They struggled to trust this God they could not see, and they complained—a lot. God sent them sweet bread from heaven every day, and instead of thanking him, they wailed for meat. In fact, they wailed so hard that Moses asked God why he had made him in charge of this group of babies, and requested that God put him to death if he was going to have to put up with them any longer (Numbers 11:10–15)! God answered by giving Moses elders to help him carry the burden, and giving the people quail to eat.

Not long after, the Israelites made another big mistake. They didn't trust God to help them take possession of the land. They were too scared! The cities were too big, and the people too powerful! They must have forgotten how big their God was. And so God made the people wander for forty years in the desert. He continued to feed them their manna and quail, and miraculously kept their clothes and shoes from wearing out. God was still saving and sanctifying his people in spite of their disobedience.

But then, you guessed it, they started to complain

again. They spoke against God and against Moses, saying, "Why have you brought us up out of Egypt to die in the wilderness? There is no bread! There is no water! And we detest this miserable food!" (Numbers 21:5).

Their problem wasn't just chronic grumbling. They were rejecting Moses and rejecting God.

So God punished them. He sent venomous snakes to the camp. The snakes bit the people, and some of them died. Immediately they knew their sin.

"Pray to the Lord that he will take the snakes away from us!" they cried. So Moses prayed.

God then did something surprising. He didn't take the snakes away, like you might expect. Instead, the snakes stayed around, but God provided a way for healing. He told Moses to make a snake and put it on a pole. Anyone who was bitten could look at the snake on the pole and live.

Moses did as he was instructed, making the snake out of bronze. He lifted the snake up in the desert, and anyone who looked at it lived.

Was the snake magic? No. Rather, when the people looked upward to the snake, they were demonstrating their trust in God to save them.

Jesus reminded Nicodemus of this story in the book of John. He said, "Just as Moses lifted up the snake in the wilderness, so the Son of Man must be lifted up, that everyone who believes may have eternal life in him" (John 3:14–15).

It seems strange at first to think that Jesus would compare himself to a snake. After all, Satan came as a serpent in the garden. But think about it this way: the bites the people experienced from the snakes were like bites of sin—poisonous sin that leads to death. Jesus, being fully God, stepped into our sinful world and became human. He was a man, but without sin, just as the bronze snake was a snake, but without poison. And Jesus, being totally perfect, was raised on a cross, much like that pole, that we who are facing death may look to him and be saved.

An unlikely method of saving, for sure, but all part of God's plan. What direction are you looking today?

# REFLECT

1. Why did God send venomous snakes into the
   Israelite camp? Do we act the same way?

2. How were the people saved? How are we saved?

3. What was Jesus talking about when he told Nicodemus "the Son
   of Man must be lifted up"? What famous verse comes right after
   this statement? How is this story a picture of God's love?

---

**BIBLE REFERENCE** NUMBERS 21:4-9

**KEY VERSE** JOHN 3:14-15

# JESUS IS THE STAR FROM JACOB AND THE SCEPTER FROM ISRAEL

"A star will come out of Jacob; a scepter will rise out of Israel."

NUMBERS 24:17

he Israelites' forty years of wandering were nearly over, and the promised land was so close! Do you remember the promises God made to Abraham? God said, "I will make you into a great nation, and I will bless you. I will make your name great and you will be a blessing. I will bless those who bless you, and whoever curses you I will curse; and all peoples on earth will be blessed through you" (Genesis 12:2–3).

God had kept these promises, and he was still keeping them and fulfilling them. And now God was about to add another promise: a victorious leader to rule his people.

Nearby, a king named Balak was watching the Israelites closely. They were numerous and scary to him. How could he stop them from attacking?

So Balak came up with a plan. He hired Balaam, a pagan sorcerer, to curse the Israelites. But God told Balaam, "No."

So Balak offered Balaam more riches, and Balaam asked God again if he could go. God said he could, but he was only allowed to do what God said.

Yes, God allowed Balaam to go, but that doesn't mean he

was happy with him. The angel of the Lord came down and stood in the road with his sword drawn, blocking the path in front of Balaam. His donkey saw the angel and ran off the road. Balaam, completely oblivious, beat the donkey and then continued on. Again the angel stood in front of them, and this time the donkey pressed close to a wall, crushing Balaam's foot. Balaam beat the donkey again. A third time the angel opposed them, and this time the donkey simply lay down, refusing to go any farther. Balaam beat the donkey again, not realizing the donkey was saving his life!

The donkey had had enough. "What have I done to you to make you beat me these three times?" it said (Numbers 22:28).

Wait a second, a talking donkey? God sure gets creative when he wants someone's attention! Balaam was probably a little shocked, but even more so, he was angry! "You've made a fool of me! If I had a sword I'd kill you right now!" he yelled. Actually, there was a sword nearby, but it was pointed at Balaam!

The donkey replied, "Am I not your own donkey, which you have always ridden, to this day? Have I been in the habit of doing this to you?" (22:30).

Then Balaam's eyes were opened and he saw the angel.

At this point you might expect Balaam to go home,

realizing the seriousness of the situation. But God allowed him to go on, because God had a plan.

Soon Balaam and Balak were making pagan sacrifices in preparation for the cursing. But when the time came, God put his words in Balaam's mouth. Instead of cursing them, Balaam blessed them!

Balak wasn't happy, and he ordered Balaam to try again, but it didn't work! Balaam said, "I have received a command to bless; he has blessed, and I cannot change it" (23:20).

The Israelites were God's treasured possession, the people he had promised to bless. And you can be sure that God keeps his promises!

By now Balak was extremely frustrated. "Change locations!" he said. "Try again!"

But Balaam continued to bless the Israelites and this time also cursed their enemies. Balak burned with anger and ordered Balaam to leave.

Balaam continued prophesying the words of God. He couldn't help it! Do you remember how God promised Abraham that all nations would be blessed through him? Balaam, the pagan, selfish sorcerer, told just how this was going to happen.

He said, "I see him, but not now; I behold him, but not near. A star will come out of Jacob; a scepter will rise out of Israel" (24:17).

Israel was going to get a king—a glorious one! But who, and when? The king is Jesus, born many years later, descended from Jacob, full of glory like a star and authority like a scepter.

God protected his people the Israelites from a curse in this story, and he protects us today from the curse of sin. How? Through Jesus, the Star and Scepter. Paul tells us in the book of Galatians: "Christ redeemed us from the curse of the law by becoming a curse for us'" (Galatians 3:13a). Jesus became the curse, defeated death, and then took his place on the throne, where he reigns today. There is no greater blessing than this.

## REFLECT

1. What two images are used in this story to point to Jesus? How do these images fit Jesus?

2. God uses a disobedient, heathen sorcerer to proclaim the coming of his Son. Does that surprise you? What might this teach us?

3. If you are a child of Abraham, and a child of God, God wants to bless YOU. And when God makes up his mind, he cannot be stopped. What comfort does this give you?

4. Read Galatians 3:13. How does this verse apply both to this story and the previous story?

5. Balak wanted Balaam to curse the Israelites, but instead he blessed them. See if you can match these verses from Balaam's oracles to the promises God made to Abraham: Numbers 23:10; Numbers 23:21; Numbers 24:5-6; Numbers 24:7; Numbers 24:9.

---

# JESUS IS OUR KINSMAN REDEEMER

In him we have redemption through his blood, the forgiveness of sins,
in accordance with the riches of God's grace that he lavished on us.

EPHESIANS 1:7-8

ave you ever been really hungry? I mean really, really hungry? Today most of us can get the food we need if our belly starts to rumble, but that was not always the case in Bible times. If there was no rain, there was no food.

This is what happened to a woman named Naomi. She lived in Bethlehem, which means "house of bread," but because of a famine, the "house of bread" was out of bread! She and her family moved to Moab, where they lived among foreign people who worshiped foreign gods. Sadly, after a time Naomi's husband died. Her sons married Moabite women, and then both of Naomi's sons died too. So Naomi was left in a foreign land with only her daughters-in-law.

"Go back to your families," Naomi said to Orpah and Ruth. She had heard that there was food once again in Israel and she wanted to go home to her people. Orpah agreed and went back to her family, but Ruth loved Naomi and clung to her.

"Where you go I will go, and where you stay I will stay.

Your people will be my people and your God my God" (Ruth 1:16b). So Ruth and Naomi set out together for Bethlehem.

Ruth and Naomi had each other but not much else. Women in that era often didn't have opportunities to find jobs or earn a living. Who would care for them? How would they get food? And what had happened to the land that once belonged to Naomi's husband? Just like us, they had needs that they couldn't meet on their own.

Well, God loves the poor, and he loves the widows. He provided for them in the laws of the Israelites. One law stated that when the Israelites were collecting the harvest, they must not collect every piece of grain. Those that were dropped and those that were on the corners of the field must be left for the poor. The poor could glean in the fields, which meant they could pick up what was left so they wouldn't go hungry.

It was the beginning of the barley harvest, and Ruth went to glean in the fields so she and Naomi could eat. She went to the field of Boaz, a kind man who followed the law of God. He took notice of Ruth and was extra kind to her because he had heard how kind she had been to her mother-in-law Naomi. He said to her, "May the LORD repay you for what you have done. May you be richly rewarded by the LORD, the God of Israel, under whose wings you have come to take refuge" (Ruth

2:12). And then he fed her a meal and made sure she had plenty of grain to glean the rest of the day.

When Ruth got home that night with a giant sack of grain, far more than any normal gleaner, Naomi couldn't believe her eyes. "Where did you glean today? Blessed be the man who took notice of you!" (Ruth 2:19).

"The name of the man I worked with today is Boaz," Ruth replied (2:19).

Then Naomi told Ruth that Boaz was one of her close relatives. Remember how God provided for the poor and the widows through his law? The law said that a close relative, or kin, could redeem the family's property by buying it back as well as marrying the widow of a deceased relative. This would restore honor to the family and allow their name and their line to continue. This was their chance! Was God providing a way for these two women? Ruth must go, Naomi explained. She must ask Boaz to be their kinsman redeemer.

And that's exactly what Ruth did. Ruth asked Boaz to spread the corner of his garment over her, which was a way of asking for his protection. She was seeking protection under the wings of the Lord, and under the care of Boaz. And Boaz, being the man of God that he was, said yes.

We too need a Kinsman Redeemer. We need to be redeemed—we have a debt of sin we cannot pay. We have been cut off from our perfect home in Eden, and we need someone to bring us back and secure our inheritance. So Jesus became our kin—he became human like us. Then he redeemed us, canceling our debt on the cross and granting us a heavenly inheritance. As our Kinsman Redeemer, Jesus provides for us, comforts us, restores us, and secures our place in his kingdom and his forever family.

# REFLECT

1. What is one way God provided for the poor and the widows in Bible times? See Leviticus 19:9–10.

2. What did Boaz do as the kinsman redeemer?

3. How is Jesus both our kin and our redeemer? See Hebrews 2:11, 17; Romans 8:17; Ephesians 1:4–8.

4. Who was Ruth's great-grandson? See Ruth 4:21–22.

5. Ruth was a foreigner, and yet she was included in the line of Jesus. Why do you think God included her? What can that teach us?

6. Who else was born in Bethlehem? See Micah 5:2 and Luke 2:4–6.

---

BIBLE REFERENCE RUTH 1-4; EPHESIANS 1:4-8

KEY VERSE EPHESIANS 1:7-8

# JESUS IS THE GREAT HIGH PRIEST

Therefore, since we have a great high priest who has ascended into heaven, Jesus the Son of God, let us hold firmly to the faith we profess.

HEBREWS 4:14

any children know the story of little Samuel. It's a sweet story, for sure. His mother Hannah wanted a son so badly, but the Lord had given her none. So she wept and she prayed, just as most women in her situation would do. But she also did something else. She made a vow. She said, "O Lord Almighty, if you will only look upon me, and not forget your servant but give her a son, then I will give him to the Lord for all the days of his life" (1 Samuel 1:11, paraphrase).

The Lord heard her prayer and her vow, and she gave birth to a son. She named him Samuel, which means, "God has heard." When he was a few years old, she brought him to Eli the high priest, where he lived and served at the tabernacle. Samuel continued to grow in stature and in favor with the Lord and men (1 Samuel 2:26).

Meanwhile, there's a not-so-sweet part of the story. The high priest's own sons, Hophni and Phinehas, were doing wicked things. God had chosen their family to serve as priests, and it was a super-special job. But they weren't treating it as something special or holy. They continued to sin, and Eli didn't stop them. Do you see how serious this was? The priests were supposed to make sacrifices for the sins of the people, and yet they refused to turn from their own sins. God sent a prophet who said the house of Eli was scorning his sacrifices. This was serious business, and there would be serious consequences. The prophet said God would cut short their days so that there would not be an old man in their family line, and Hophni and Phinehas would die on the same day.

This was terrible news for Eli and his family. And yet God gave a glimmer of hope by making a promise through this prophet. God would raise up a faithful priest, who would minister forever.

One night the Lord called to Samuel. Three times the boy ran to Eli because he thought it was Eli calling him, but it wasn't—it was God! The first two times Eli told him to go back to bed, but the third time he realized it was the Lord. Eli told him to lie back down, and if the Lord called again to say, "Speak, LORD, for your servant is listening" (1 Samuel 3:9).

Samuel did as Eli told him, and the Lord told Samuel that he was about to carry out the prophecy against Eli and his family.

Samuel was afraid to tell Eli the vision, but when Eli pressed him, he told him everything. Eli said, "He is the LORD; let him do what is good in his eyes" (3:18).

Not long after this night, the Israelites went out to fight the Philistines. Hophni and Phinehas moved the ark into the battlefield, which they were not supposed to do. God allowed the ark to be captured by the Philistines, and Hophni and Phinehas were killed.

God's punishment for these priests who weren't following his will was serious. This shows us again that the job of priest was an important one. It was through the priest that sacrifices were made as payment for sins, and it needed to be done right. The problem was that the priests themselves were imperfect, and needed to make sacrifices for themselves before they could make sacrifices for the people. God did raise up a faithful priest as he promised, whose name was Zadok, but even he wasn't absolutely perfect, and he couldn't possibly live forever. So what was the solution? And why don't we have priests and sacrifices anymore?

The solution is Jesus. He is the perfect High Priest. He's sinless, and he's eternal. And do you know what? He's the sacrifice too! Jesus fulfills all God's requirements. No more sacrifices need to be made. When Jesus was on the cross, he said, "It is finished" (John 19:30). Jesus, our Great High Priest, made the final sacrifice—himself.

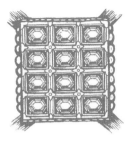

# REFLECT

1. What was the job of the priests?

2. According to Hebrews 4:14-16, why is Jesus the Great High Priest?

3. Read the story of Melchizedek in Genesis 14:18-20 and Hebrews 7:1-10. What two roles did Melchizedek and Jesus both have?

---

**BIBLE REFERENCE** 1 SAMUEL 1-3; HEBREWS 4:14-16

**KEY VERSE** HEBREWS 4:14

# JESUS IS THE SON OF DAVID

---

*"You will conceive and give birth to a son, and you are to call him Jesus. He will be great and will be called the Son of the Most High. The Lord God will give him the throne of his father David, and he will reign over Jacob's descendants forever; his kingdom will never end."*

LUKE 1:31-33

avid is probably one of the best-known characters in the Bible. David was the handsome shepherd boy, handpicked by God and anointed by Samuel, even though he was the youngest boy in the family. He's the boy who had the confidence to face Goliath with just a sling and a stone, and he won! He was talented in many ways: tending sheep, fighting off bears and lions, and even playing the harp. He's the writer of many songs, which we find in our Bibles in the book of Psalms and still sing today. David was also a brave warrior, commanding mighty men and winning countless victories. He was a man of great faith. When King Saul wanted to kill him, David didn't take matters into his own hands, but instead he cried out to God for salvation, trusting that God would make him king when the time was right. And when he messed up—as he did in very serious ways—he always repented and asked for God's forgiveness. He had a very close relationship with God, and God called him "a man after his own heart" (1 Samuel 13:14).

Because David loved God deeply, something bothered him as he sat in his palace. "Here I am, living in a house of cedar," he said, "while the ark of God remains in a tent" (2 Samuel 7:2). David wanted to build a beautiful house for God.

If we were the writers of God's story, we would probably say, "Yes, build God a big, beautiful house! A magnificent one!" But God didn't say yes. God said no. David was a man of war. He had shed too much blood. He could not build God a house, but his son Solomon would instead.

We can imagine David's disappointment as he heard this. But then God said something surprising—something amazing. David was not allowed to build a house for God, but God was going to build a house for David! No, not a house of wood or of stone, but a house of people. A house of kings; many of them. God said David's throne would be established forever.

David was amazed at God's love. "Who am I, Sovereign LORD, and what is my family, that you have brought me this far? And as if this were not enough in your sight, Sovereign LORD, you have also spoken about the future of the house of your servant—and this decree, Sovereign LORD, is for a mere human!" (7:18–19).

David's line continued through the years, with kings and more kings, some good and some bad. But would his line really last forever? Would someone from David's family always reign on the throne? And really, the people may have wondered, who could ever be a king as great as David? Who could possibly rescue God's people from their enemies as well as David? Who could rule so justly? Who could bring peace once again? The years went by and the people wondered.

But then a king was born. He wasn't born in a palace, so not everyone paid attention, but he was indeed from the line of David, and even the town of Bethlehem, just like David! He didn't sit on a throne in Israel, as they may have expected or hoped, but he is reigning today on his throne in heaven, and will reign for eternity. He's our rescuer from sin, the victor over our enemies, the Great Shepherd, and the Prince of Peace. He's more than just the man after God's own heart, because he and God are one. His name is Jesus!

# REFLECT

1. Read Luke 1:30-33. What did the angel promise Mary?

2. What similarities are there between David and Jesus?

3. How is Jesus a better king than David?

4. Read Genesis 49:10. Who is talking? Who is he talking about? How does it relate to today's story?

---

**BIBLE REFERENCE** 2 SAMUEL 7

**KEY VERSE** LUKE 1:31-33

# JESUS IS OUR GREAT PROPHET

They were all filled with awe and praised God. "A great prophet has appeared among us," they said. "God has come to help his people."

LUKE 7:16

In Old Testament times, people didn't hear from God the way we do today. There wasn't a Bible available in each home to read the words of God, and they didn't have the Holy Spirit to guide them. Instead, God spoke to the people through his prophets. God would give his word to the prophet, and the prophet would deliver the message to the people. Often the message was something like, "Stop sinning! Turn back to me!"

One of the best-known prophets was Elijah. Elijah lived during the time when God's people had split into two kingdoms, Israel and Judah. God sent Elijah to speak to Ahab, king of Israel, who was a wicked man. Ahab wanted God's people to worship false gods like Baal and Asherah. The Bible says he did more to make God angry than any of the kings before him.

Elijah said to Ahab, "As the LORD, the God of Israel, lives, whom I serve, there will be neither dew nor rain in the next few years except at my word" (1 Kings 17:1). This was bad news for King Ahab. No rain meant no crops, and no crops meant no food.

God sent Elijah away to hide from Ahab's anger. God took care of Elijah by giving him water to drink from a brook, and he sent ravens to bring him bread and meat. When the brook dried up, God sent him to a widow's house. The widow and her son were nearly starving, but they were kind to Elijah and shared their little bit of food with him. God blessed them and took care of them, and their flour jar and oil jug never ran out, so they always had a little bit of bread to eat.

One day the widow's son became sick. He got worse and worse, and finally he stopped breathing. Elijah cried out to the Lord, praying for his life to return. God heard Elijah's cry, and the boy was raised from the dead!

Not long after this miracle, God showed his power once again. God sent fire from heaven to prove that he—not Baal—was the one, true, powerful God. God used the ministry and obedience of Elijah to rescue his people from idolatry and turn them back to him. And because he's gracious and forgiving, he sent rain too.

When Jesus was on earth, he, too, raised a widow's son from the dead. When the people saw it they said, "A great prophet has appeared among us. God has come to help his people" (Luke 7:16).

They were right—Jesus was a great prophet! He was far greater than Elijah or any other prophet. And he was coming to help God's people turn back to him, though they didn't fully understand how. And yet he was more than just a great prophet. Listen carefully to this: John tells us that Jesus not only brings the Word, but he *is* the Word. Jesus is the only way we can be freed from our sins and turn back to God.

# REFLECT

1. What was the job of a prophet?

2. What does it mean that Jesus is the Word? See John 1:1-5.

3. How is Jesus our great prophet? See Hebrews 1:1-3.

---

**BIBLE REFERENCE** 1 KINGS 17; LUKE 7:11-17

**KEY VERSE** LUKE 7:16

# JESUS IS
# GREATER
# THAN JONAH

"For as Jonah was three days and three nights in the belly of a huge fish, so the Son of Man will be three days and three nights in the heart of the earth."

MATTHEW 12:40

oday we meet another prophet in the Old Testament. His name is Jonah. Like Elijah, his job was to tell people to stop sinning and turn back to God. But unlike Elijah, God told Jonah to talk to the Ninevites, not the Israelites. Who were the Ninevites? They were enemies of God's people—major enemies. They lived in the huge city of Ninevah, and were known for their big armies and cruel, wicked plans.

*Why should I preach to those scoundrels?* Jonah thought.

*Why should God be compassionate to them when they are so terrible?*

So Jonah hopped on a ship headed in the opposite direction. He was trying to hide from the Lord, which, of course, is impossible.

The Lord sent a great wind on the sea and a violent storm arose. All the sailors were super scared that their ship would break apart and they would drown. Jonah, meanwhile, was sleeping in the bottom of the ship.

"Wake up!" the captain said. "Pray to your god like the rest of us are doing! We need help! We're going to die!"

The sailors cast lots, which was like throwing dice, to see whose fault the storm was. The lot pointed to Jonah. He told them who he was, and how he was running from the God who made the land and the sea.

The storm was getting worse. "Pick me up and throw me into the sea!" Jonah said. "Then it will become calm and you will live! I know this is my fault!"

The sailors didn't want Jonah to die, so they did their best to row, but the waves became even more wild. So with a cry to the Lord, they threw Jonah overboard. Instantly the raging sea grew calm. The sailors were amazed and fearful. They offered sacrifices to the Lord and made promises to him.

But what happened to Jonah? Did he die? Almost. But God, the Creator of the seas, had an epic rescue plan. He commanded a great fish to swallow Jonah. Jonah stayed in the belly of the fish for three days, praying to the Lord and waiting to see what would happen to him. It felt like death to Jonah, and yet he had some amount of hope. He ended his prayer with the words, "Salvation comes from the LORD" (Jonah 2:9).

Then the Lord spoke to the fish, and it vomited Jonah onto dry land. He was saved!

God spoke to Jonah again: "Go to the great city of Nineveh and proclaim to it the message I give you" (3:2). This time Jonah obeyed. He went to Nineveh and spoke to these people he hated, telling them to stop being wicked, or in forty days they would be destroyed. Word spread all the way to the king, and he ordered everyone in the kingdom to stop eating and pray to Jonah's God. When God saw their repentance, he had compassion on them and did not destroy them.

In the New Testament we read about another violent storm. This time it's Jesus and his disciples who are in the boat. Again, the waves are high and threaten to sink the ship. And who is asleep in the bottom of the boat? Jesus. The disciples wake him up saying, "We're going to die!"

Jesus is greater than Jonah. He created the sea, so the sea must obey his every word. "Quiet!" he commanded. "Be still!" Instantly the raging sea was calm. Like the men in Jonah's story, the disciples were amazed and fearful.

Jesus didn't go overboard into the sea like Jonah to save the sailors. At least not literally, and not at that moment. But he did something greater. Jesus sank deep into death to save them—to save all of us, whether we are sailors, Israelites, Ninevites, or whoever. How much greater is Jesus than Jonah!

Yes, Jonah sank into the sea and spent three days in the belly of the fish. Many years later Jesus died on the cross and spent three days in the tomb. Then, at the Lord's command, the grave opened and Jesus rose from the dead. The story of Jonah is a sign pointing us to Jesus, whose name means, "He saves." With Jonah we can say, "Salvation comes from the Lord!"

# REFLECT

1. How is Jesus like Jonah? Think about the story of Jesus calming the storm as well as his time in the grave.

2. How is Jesus greater than Jonah?

3. The people of the Bible thought of the sea as a scary place—a place of chaos, disorder, and even death. Read Psalms 18:16; 32:6; 65:5-7; 74:13-14; and 107:28-30. Who rules the sea? Do you think the disciples thought of these passages when Jesus calmed the storm, and what did that reveal to them?

4. Who has salvation been made available to? See Revelation 5:9.

---

**BIBLE REFERENCE** JONAH 1-4;
MARK 4:35-41; MATTHEW 8:23-27; 12:38-41

**KEY VERSE** MATTHEW 12:40

# JESUS IS THE HORN OF OUR SALVATION

"Praise be to the Lord, the God of Israel, because he has come to his people and redeemed them. He has raised up a horn of salvation for us in the house of his servant David."

LUKE 1:68-69

any years had passed, and God's people were still looking for a Savior, the Messiah they had been promised. Where was he? God's people had been captured, ruled, and oppressed by the Assyrians, Babylonians, Persians, and Romans. When would they finally be free? They wanted a mighty king to be born, to win them victories in battle and take his rightful place on the throne. Without a king they felt powerless.

In the meantime, faithful believers continued to wait and worship, including an old priest named Zechariah.

One day Zechariah was chosen by lot to burn incense in the temple. It was a job that a priest didn't get picked for very often, if ever. Zechariah was probably full of emotion—excited, nervous, and maybe even a little scared. He was going to be so close to the Presence of God! This was a day he would surely remember for the rest of his life.

But little did he know how significant this day would be for him, for his whole nation, and for the whole world. God had a big surprise—*the Messiah was coming soon!*

Zechariah walked in, and there, standing at the right side of the altar of incense, was an angel! Zechariah was super scared!

"Do not be afraid, Zechariah," the angel said. "Your wife Elizabeth will bear you a son, and you are to call him John. . . . He will go on before the Lord, in the spirit and power of Elijah . . . to make ready a people prepared for the Lord" (Luke 1:13, 17).

Zechariah asked the angel for a sign that he could be sure this would happen. After all, he and his wife were very old and had never had children!

But the angel answered, "I am Gabriel. I stand in the presence of God, and I have been sent to speak to you and to tell you this good news. And now you will be silent and not able to speak until the day this happens, because you did not believe my words" (1:19–20).

Zechariah came out of the temple and was supposed to give a blessing, but he couldn't even speak! All through Elizabeth's pregnancy, Zechariah was silent. He had lots of time to think, to wonder, and to meditate on God's Word as he awaited his precious son. What the angel had said was true! This was the turning point in history, the time God's people had been waiting for, what the prophets had foretold, and he was a part of it!

At last, the baby arrived. Elizabeth named him John and everyone was confused. It was not a family name.

So they made signs to Zechariah, asking what he would like to name the child.

Zechariah simply wrote, "His name is John." Suddenly Zechariah was able to speak and he began praising God, filled with the Holy Spirit. Everyone was amazed.

"Praise be to the Lord, the God of Israel," prophesied Zechariah, "because he has come to his people and redeemed them. He has raised up a horn of salvation for us in the house of his servant David" (Luke 1:68–69).

What did he mean by a "horn of salvation"? The horn he was talking about was not a trumpet, but the horn of a wild ox, a deadly weapon, and a symbol of incredible power and victory.[2] Zechariah was borrowing the symbol from David who said, "LORD, surely your enemies will perish. . . . You have exalted my horn like that of a wild ox" (Psalm 92:9–10). David called God "the horn of my salvation" because he knew he was safe with God on his side (Psalm 18:2).

Zechariah was using the same imagery, calling the coming Messiah the horn of salvation. Jesus would have incredible power to conquer Israel's enemies, freeing them at last. Zechariah's own son John would prepare the way for Jesus by teaching repentance.

We don't know how Zechariah pictured all this happening. Jesus wasn't coming to battle the Romans as many of the Jews expected him to, but to battle even greater enemies—sin, death, and the curse. The battle was so much bigger and significant than they realized! But

Zechariah was absolutely right that Jesus is strong like the horn of an ox. He's strong enough to crush the head of the serpent and defeat death forever. We are absolutely safe and secure with Jesus, the Horn of our Salvation, on our side. Blessed be the Lord God of Israel!

# REFLECT

1. Read Romans 5:6-8. How do these verses describe us in our sin?

2. Look up a picture of a wild ox. How is Jesus like an ox's horn?

3. Read Psalm 18:2. How did God keep David safe? How does he keep you safe in this life and in the life to come? See also Psalm 92:9-10 and 2 Samuel 22:3.

---

**BIBLE REFERENCE** LUKE 1:5-25, 57-80

**KEY VERSE** LUKE 1:68-69

# JESUS IS THE PRINCE OF PEACE

---

"For to us a child is born, to us a son is given, and the government will be on his shoulders. And he will be called Wonderful Counselor, Mighty God, Everlasting Father, Prince of Peace."

ISAIAH 9:6

ong before Jesus's birth, God sent out an announcement through the prophet Isaiah. This birth announcement didn't tell how many pounds or how many inches he was, but it did describe him in other ways. This is what Isaiah said: "For to us a child is born, to us a son is given, and the government will be on his shoulders. And he will be called Wonderful Counselor, Mighty God, Everlasting Father, Prince of Peace" (9:6).

Not many babies get four names! Especially not four important names, and names used for God himself!

Isaiah is telling us without a doubt that this baby is God, come to live among his people. God the King was sending down his Son, the Prince of Peace. This was a royal announcement!

Many years later an angel visited a young woman named Mary, giving her surprising news. "You will conceive and give birth to a son, and you are to call him Jesus. He will be great and will be called the Son of the Most High. The Lord God will give him the throne of his father David, and he will reign over Jacob's descendants forever; his kingdom will never end" (Luke 1:31–33).

Until this moment, Mary had no clue she was going to be a mother, much less a mother of a prince. Mary wasn't a queen, and she didn't live in a castle. She wasn't even wealthy! She must have wondered how she would raise the son of the King of kings. But Mary trusted God with the details. "I am the Lord's servant," Mary answered. "May your word to me be fulfilled" (Luke 1:38).

Nothing went as Mary, or you, or I would have expected. The baby came while Mary and Joseph were traveling, and the only place they had to lay him down was in a manger, a feedbox for animals. Their surroundings were probably dirty and smelly. Instead of royal robes, this little prince was simply wrapped in strips of cloth.

But this was just how God had planned it, and he was taking care of the royal details. On a hillside nearby, some ordinary shepherds were about to get the most spectacular birth announcement ever delivered. An angel appeared to them, saying, "Today in the town of David a Savior has been born to you; he is the Messiah, the Lord" (Luke 2:11)!

Then suddenly with the angel appeared an entire army of angels, praising God together saying, "Glory to God in the highest heaven, and on earth *peace* to those on whom his favor rests" (Luke 2:14, emphasis mine).

The shepherds ran off and found Mary, Joseph, and little baby Jesus, who was right in the manger where the angel told them he would be. The shepherds couldn't contain their excitement.

Sometime later, wise men came from the east, following an unusual star. They knew that this star meant the king of the Jews had been born, and they set out to find him.

When the star led them to the right house, they were so happy! They saw Mary and Jesus, and they bowed down and worshiped the little king. Then they gave him gold, frankincense, and myrrh—valuable treasures fit for royalty.

Whether or not they realized it, Jesus was their king too! Jesus is king of the whole universe, and yet he came as a baby, entering our filthy, sinful world to bring us peace with God. He would be buried in a tomb, wrapped with strips of cloth and sweet-smelling myrrh. Then he would rise again with victory to sit on his forever throne as forever king, bringing everlasting peace to the earth. The Prince of Peace had arrived!

# REFLECT

1. The shepherds and wise men weren't quiet about their joy in seeing Jesus. Matthew 2:10 (ESV) says the wise men "rejoiced exceedingly with great joy," and the shepherds wanted to spread the word about him. Are you rejoicing exceedingly with great joy over the Prince of Peace? Are you spreading the word?

2. Reflect on Isaiah 9:6–7. How do you think his government and peace will continue to increase?

3. How are we filled with the peace of God? See Romans 15:13.

---

BIBLE REFERENCE MATTHEW 2:1–12; LUKE 2:1–20

KEY VERSE ISAIAH 9:6

# JESUS IS THE SON OF GOD

And a voice from heaven said, "This is my Son,
whom I love; with him I am well pleased."

MATTHEW 3:17

ave you ever wondered what Jesus was like as a little boy? The Bible doesn't tell us a lot about his growing-up years, other than that he "grew in wisdom and stature, and in favor with God and man" (Luke 2:52). In other words, he matured like other boys, and he was obedient. But unlike other boys, he was completely sinless, perfectly pleasing both his earthly parents and his heavenly Father.

Jesus's cousin John was the one God chose to prepare the way for Jesus. John was a unique character, living

in the desert, wearing camel skins, and eating locusts and wild honey. He began preaching near the Jordan River, telling the people they must turn away from their sins and turn back to God. Many people listened, and John baptized them.

As John's popularity spread, people began to wonder and ask who he was. Was he the Messiah, the one they were waiting for?

"No!" answered John. He was just the one preparing the way. He was trying to help them see their sin and their

89

need for a Savior. "Someone else is coming after me," he said. "I'm not even special enough to untie his shoes."

One day Jesus came down to the Jordan River. He wanted to be baptized by John. But John tried to stop him. "I need to be baptized by you, and you're coming to me?"

But Jesus said this was the right thing to do, so John agreed. John baptized Jesus, and as soon as Jesus rose up out of the water, the heavens opened. The Spirit of God came down like a dove and rested on him. A voice from heaven said, "This is my Son, whom I love; with him I am well pleased" (Matthew 3:17).

Now John knew without a doubt that his cousin Jesus was the Son of God.

After this, the Spirit of God led Jesus to the desert for forty days and forty nights. Someone came who knew exactly who Jesus was, and he wasn't happy about it. It was the devil. The devil knew if he could get Jesus to sin, then God's whole plan would be ruined. He had gotten Adam and Eve to sin all those many years ago, and now was his chance to tempt the very Son of God.

Jesus hadn't eaten for a long time, and he was very hungry, so the devil said, "If you are the Son of God, tell these stones to become bread" (Matthew 4:3).

Jesus wasn't going to listen to him. Instead, he quoted a verse from Deuteronomy. "It is written: 'Man shall not live on bread alone, but on every word that comes from the mouth of God'" (Matthew 4:4).

So the devil tried again. He took Jesus to the highest point of the temple and said, "Throw yourself down. The Scriptures say the angels will catch you."

Jesus answered him, "The Scriptures also say, 'Do not put the Lord your God to the test'" (Matthew 4:7 paraphrase).

The devil tried once more. He took Jesus to a very high mountain and showed him all the kingdoms and riches of the world. "This can all be yours," he said, "if you bow down and worship me."

But the devil was not going to win. He could not make Jesus sin. "Away from me, Satan! For it is written: 'Worship the Lord your God, and serve him only'" (4:10).

So the devil left, and God sent angels to care for his Son Jesus and strengthen him. It was time for Jesus to start his ministry. He had God's fullest approval and blessing, he was anointed and empowered with the Holy Spirit, and the devil wasn't going to stop him. He was God's Son.

# REFLECT

1. Name the three persons of the Trinity and describe how we see them in the story of Jesus's baptism.

2. Read Isaiah 42:1. How does this story fulfill Isaiah's prophecy?

3. Why is it so important that Jesus was sinless? See 2 Corinthians 5:21 and Hebrews 4:15.

4. In Luke's gospel, he inserts a genealogy of Jesus between his baptism and temptation. Read Luke 3:38. What is Adam called? How are Jesus and Adam different? See also 1 Corinthians 15:45–49.

---

**BIBLE REFERENCE** ISAIAH 42:1; MATTHEW 3:13–4:11

**KEY VERSE** MATTHEW 3:17

# JESUS IS THE MIRACLE WORKER

You are the God who performs miracles;
you display your power among the peoples.

PSALM 77:14

ollowing his baptism and temptation, Jesus chose twelve disciples to follow him. These twelve men left their jobs, their homes, and their families to follow their rabbi. Little did they know what they would see and hear in the coming days and weeks, and how their minds and hearts would change.

Jesus and his disciples were invited to a wedding in Cana. The bride and groom were probably close family friends or relatives of Jesus, since his mother and brothers were there as well. Jesus's mother, Mary, came to him with a major problem: there was no more wine!

Now, at first this might not seem like a big deal. Just drink something else, right? Well, no. In Jesus's time people drank mostly water and wine. And a wedding is a celebration, so you need wine. If a host were to run out of wine, it was considered a serious offense and brought shame to the family. Not only that, but wedding feasts sometimes lasted for days, so someone needed to get more wine, and fast!

Jesus said to his mother, "Why do you involve me? My hour has not yet come" (John 2:4).

But Mary, knowing who her son was, told the servants, "Do whatever he tells you" (2:5).

Nearby were six huge stone jars. Each of them could hold twenty to thirty gallons of water. They were there because Jews used jars like these for ceremonial washing, following the Jewish law.

Jesus told the servants, "Fill the jars with water" (2:7).

And the servants did, all the way to the top.

Then Jesus told them to pour some and take it to the master of the banquet.

The master tasted the most delicious wine, and he asked the groom, "Why are you serving this wine now? Everyone else serves the best first, and saves the cheap stuff for when their guests have had their fill. You've saved the best for last!"

We don't know what the groom answered, but we can imagine he stuttered something in his astonishment. Word probably got out pretty quickly from the servants, and the wedding was abuzz with the news of this miracle. The wine flowed freely, for there was much of it, and Jesus restored honor to this family.

Jesus revealed his glory through this first miracle, and as a result his disciples believed in him.

Perhaps they knew the prophecy from Joel, that when the day of the Lord came, the day the Messiah would appear, the mountains would drip with new wine (Joel 2:1; 3:18). Imagine their joy and their thought process: *Is the day of the Lord here? He made water turn to wine! And so much—120 gallons! He has power over nature! Could he be the Messiah? He must be! We better listen and follow!*

Oh, how much more they would see! This was only the beginning of Jesus's ministry.

# REFLECT

1. Why do you think Jesus responded to his mother the way he did, and then did the miracle?

2. Jesus used jars intended for ceremonial washing for wine (John 2:6). How might this show the change between the old covenant and the new covenant?

3. How have you seen Jesus as the miracle worker in your own life?

---

**BIBLE REFERENCE** JOHN 2:1–11

**KEY VERSE** PSALM 77:14

# JESUS IS THE CLEANSER

"On that day a fountain will be opened to the house of David and the inhabitants of Jerusalem, to cleanse them from sin and impurity."

ZECHARIAH 13:1

t was almost time for the Passover, so Jesus and his disciples went up to Jerusalem. They were not alone. Many Jews went to Jerusalem for the Passover celebration, remembering how God delivered them from Egypt. High on the hill of Jerusalem stood the temple. It was the house of God, and for Jesus, it was his Father's house, the copy and shadow of his heavenly home here on earth. Imagine how Jesus felt as he walked up to his Father's house.

But oh, the sight he found there! In the temple courts Jesus saw men selling cattle, sheep, and doves. More men sat at tables exchanging money. It was like a giant flea market. Instead of praying and worshiping, people were buying and selling to make a profit! This outer court of the temple was supposed to be the area where Gentiles could come to pray, but with everything going on, how could they? What a mess!

Jesus did not want his Father's house to be treated as a marketplace, so he made a whip out of cords, and he drove the sellers and their animals out. He overturned the tables of the money changers and scattered their coins. Imagine the surprise, the yelling of angry sellers, the mooing of the cattle, and the bleating of the sheep.

"Get these out of here!" he said. "Stop turning my Father's house into a market!" (John 2:16).

The disciples, who knew their Scriptures well, remembered the words of David the psalmist, "Zeal for your house will consume me" (2:17). Here was another clue for them that Jesus was the Messiah. Jesus, who loved his Father's house, was cleaning it up.

The Jews were probably startled, outraged, and confused. Who was this man, and what did he think he was doing? They asked him, "What sign can you show us to prove your authority to do all this?" (2:18).

But Jesus didn't give them a miraculous sign. At least not one they would be able to make sense of yet. He said, "Destroy this temple, and I will raise it again in three days" (2:19).

What? It had taken forty-six years to build the temple! How could one man build it in three days?

But Jesus wasn't talking about the physical temple. He was talking about himself. His body was the temple. They would kill him, and three days later, he would rise again.

Jesus was on a cleansing mission. The cleansing of the temple was needed for sure, but his ultimate mission was to cleanse hearts. When his body, his temple, was crucified, our hearts were made clean and pure through the washing of his blood. And now we can be a temple for his Spirit to dwell.

# REFLECT

1. Why do you think Jesus reacted the way he did?
Is it okay for us to be angry about certain things?

2. Jesus cleaned the temple before Passover, and meanwhile the Jewish people were cleaning all the yeast out of their houses to prepare for Passover. What did yeast represent, and how might this relate to our story? See 1 Corinthians 5:6-8.

3. How does Jesus clean us and make us pure?

4. Read 1 Corinthians 6:19-20. How can we keep God's temple clean?

---

**BIBLE REFERENCE** JOHN 2:12-22

**KEY VERSE** ZECHARIAH 13:1

# JESUS IS THE LIVING WATER

Jesus answered her, "If you knew the gift of God and who it is that asks you for a drink, you would have asked him and he would have given you living water."

JOHN 4:10

ne day Jesus and his disciples were on their way from Judea to Galilee. Most Jews in Bible times would cross the Jordan River to avoid traveling through a place called Samaria. This would take more time, of course, but the Jews hated the people of Samaria and preferred to avoid them completely. Jesus, however, ignored this idea and purposefully traveled through Samaria.

It was the middle of the day, and Jesus, being fully human, was hot and tired from the journey. He sent the disciples into town to buy food and sat down on the edge of a well to rest. This happened to be a well dug by a long-ago ancestor of Jesus named Jacob. Remember him?

A Samaritan woman came to the well to draw water. Jesus said to her, "Will you give me a drink?" (John 4:7).

The Samaritan woman was surprised. This was a Jewish man, and she was a Samaritan woman. They could certainly not share a drinking cup. That would be considered unclean to a Jew. "How can you ask me for a drink?" she said (4:9). Little did she know who this poor, weary traveler in front of her was.

Jesus answered her, "If you knew the gift of God and who it is that asks you for a drink, you would have asked him and he would have given you living water" (4:10).

Now the woman was really confused. He didn't have anything to draw water with, and the well was really, really deep. How was he going to get this living water?

She asked him, "Are you greater than our father Jacob, who gave us the well and drank from it himself?" (4:12).

Jesus answered, "Everyone who drinks this water will be thirsty again, but whoever drinks the water I give them will never thirst. Indeed, the water I give them will become in them a spring of water welling up to eternal life" (4:13–14).

The woman wanted this water. She didn't want to have to keep coming to the well every day to get water. She was eager, but she wasn't understanding. Jesus wasn't talking about normal water.

So Jesus steered the conversation in a different direction. He told her things he knew about her and her life and how she was living in sin. He showed her how

much she needed this living water.

*How did he know these things?* she wondered. Now she was convinced he was not only greater than Jacob, but a prophet as well. Jesus continued to pursue her heart and then revealed to her that he was the Messiah.

At that moment the disciples returned and were surprised to see him talking alone with a woman. The woman left her water jar at the well and ran to town to tell the people what had just happened. "Come, see a man who told me everything I ever did," she said. "Could this be the Messiah?" (4:29).

The people of the town believed in Jesus because of the woman's testimony, and they begged Jesus to stay and teach them. They became convinced that Jesus was the Savior of the world.

Later at the Feast of Tabernacles in Jerusalem, Jesus stood and said in a loud voice, "Let anyone who is thirsty come to me and drink. Whoever believes in me, as the Scripture has said, rivers of living water will flow from within them" (John 7:37–38).

Jesus was pointing the people back to the words of the prophets, who spoke of God as a fountain of living waters (Jeremiah 2:13). Isaiah said, "The LORD will guide you always; he will satisfy your needs in a sun-scorched land and strengthen your frame. You will be like a well-watered garden, like a spring whose waters never fail" (58:11). When we come to Jesus, the Son of God, the source of living water, we will be completely satisfied. We will never thirst again, and we will have the waters of his Spirit leaping up in our souls to eternal life.

# REFLECT

1. Have you ever been *really* thirsty? What was it like? Consider the climate of Israel and the availability of water in Bible times. What do you think it meant to the people of Jesus's day that they would *never* thirst again?

2. Jesus revealed to the Samaritan woman that he was the Messiah. She's the only person recorded in Scripture that he specifically says this to until his trial. Why do you think this is?

3. What is the source of the river of the water of life? See Revelation 22:1.

4. What price must we pay for this water? See Isaiah 55:1 and Revelation 21:6; 22:17.

5. What does God's voice sound like? See Ezekiel 43:2 and Revelation 1:15.

---

**BIBLE REFERENCE** JOHN 4:1-42; 7:37-38

**KEY VERSE** JOHN 4:10

# JESUS IS
# THE BREAD
# OF LIFE

---

Then Jesus declared, "I am the bread of life. Whoever comes to me will
never go hungry, and whoever believes in me will never be thirsty."

JOHN 6:35

 esus was starting to become pretty popular. Crowds followed him, hoping to see more miraculous signs. They wondered if he could do something amazing for them too.

It was almost time for the Passover and the Feast of Unleavened Bread, when the Israelites celebrated their deliverance from Egypt. It was a time of looking back, but also a time of looking forward. They knew another prophet was coming, and they sure were sick of those Romans ruling over them.

Jesus looked up and saw a great crowd coming toward him, more than five thousand people. He said to Philip, "Where shall we buy bread for these people to eat?" (John 6:5). It wasn't that Jesus didn't know what to do, but he said this to test his disciples.

The disciples thought this was an impossible task. They didn't have enough money to feed all these people. They found a boy with five small loaves of bread and two little fish, but really, how could that help?

Jesus told the disciples to have the people sit down.

Then he took the boy's bread, gave thanks, and passed it out to the people. He did the same with the fish. Everyone had enough to eat, and there were even twelve baskets of leftovers!

The people were amazed and said, "Surely this is the Prophet who is to come into the world" (John 6:14).

They should make him king! He could heal people and he could give them bread, just like Moses! Maybe he was the one who would free them from the Romans and make their lives easy again!

Jesus knew what they were thinking and withdrew to a mountain by himself. Evening came, and the disciples got in a boat to sail to Capernaum. A storm came, and the seas became rough. Suddenly they saw Jesus walking on the water toward them. They were frightened, but Jesus assured them, and they took him in the boat. Immediately the boat reached the shore.

The next day everyone was confused. How did Jesus get to the other side of the lake? He didn't leave with the disciples. So they asked him.

Jesus answered, "Very truly I tell you, you are looking for me, not because you saw the signs I performed but because you ate the loaves and had your fill" (6:26).

Jesus knew they were coming because they wanted physical things. They wanted food, health, freedom, and prosperity. But Jesus hadn't come to fill their bellies; he had come to fill their souls and save them from their sins. The people desired more bread, but Jesus wanted them to desire *him*!

The people asked for another sign, and still thinking about bread, they reminded him of the manna in the desert. "Do a miracle like that!" they begged.

Jesus then said to them, "Truly, truly I say to you, it was not Moses who gave you the bread from heaven, but my Father gives you the true bread from heaven. For the bread of God is he who comes down from heaven and gives life to the world" (John 6:32–33 ESV).

"Sir, give us this bread always," they said (6:34 ESV).

Jesus said to them, "I am the bread of life. Whoever comes to me will never go hungry, and whoever believes in me will never be thirsty" (6:35).

But the people didn't get it. They grumbled about what he said, wondering how he could say he had come down from heaven. Didn't they know his parents?

They continued to argue, and Jesus continued to teach them. "Very truly I tell you, unless you eat the flesh of the Son of Man and drink his blood, you have no life in you" (John 6:53). What? How could they possibly eat his flesh? This sounded crazy to them, and many followers turned away.

But Jesus was indeed the bread from heaven. He was the Bread of Life, born in Bethlehem, the "house of bread." And the night before his death he would offer his disciples the Passover bread, saying, "This is my body, broken for you. Eat it in remembrance of me" (Luke 22:19, paraphrase).

You see, Jesus wants us to desire him like we desire food. Jesus, the Bread of Life, can satisfy our souls. When we want him, crave him, depend on him, and believe in him—it is then that we receive life.[3]

# REFLECT

1. List all the Bible stories you can think of involving bread. How might they point us to Jesus?

2. Have you ever made bread from scratch? It's a lot of work! Read Genesis 3:19. (Note that some translations say "bread" and some say "food.") We have it pretty easy, but for most of human history, people have had to work very hard to make their daily bread. What work must we do to receive Jesus as our bread? See John 6:27–29.

3. What are we doing when we celebrate the Lord's Supper today? See 1 Corinthians 11:23–26.

4. Do an online search for Passover bread. What does it look like? How might it point us to Jesus? See Isaiah 53:5.

BIBLE REFERENCE JOHN 6:1–59

KEY VERSE JOHN 6:35

# JESUS IS THE LIGHT OF THE WORLD

"I am the light of the world. Whoever follows me will never walk in darkness, but will have the light of life."

JOHN 8:12

hree times a year God's people went to Jerusalem for a festival. Perhaps the most exciting for children was the Feast of Tabernacles, which celebrated how God brought them out of Egypt to live in tabernacles. It was a celebration of freedom, and because of the time of year, it was a celebration of the harvest as well.

What would be more fun than living in a tent in the big city of Jerusalem with your family for an entire week? You got to travel, build a tent, decorate it, feast in it, and sleep in it. And the law given in Leviticus was clear: you must rejoice!

Jewish history tells us that the people added even more to the feast on top of God's commands.[4] One part was called the water-drawing ceremony. A priest would go down to the pool of Siloam and fill a golden pitcher with water. Then with great rejoicing, he would carry it to the temple and pour it out on the altar, thanking God for the rains. The people paraded behind, playing flutes, waving palm branches, and shouting, "LORD, save us! LORD, grant us success!" (Psalm 118:25). This happened every day of the feast, growing in intensity and celebration.

The Jews also added a light show. Four giant pillars stood in the temple courtyard, each seventy-five feet tall with four branches coming out like a lampstand. The priests used their old garments as wicks and carried gallons of oil up a ladder to light the lamps. All through the night the people would celebrate, dancing with torches and singing to the Lord. The lamps and torches lit up the whole city of Jerusalem, and the golden temple must have glowed. The people were reminded of the glory of the Lord in the pillar of fire in the wilderness, and they rejoiced.

The events of the Feast of Tabernacles were so popular and so fun, that it has been said, "Anyone who has not seen it has not seen true joy in his life!"[5]

Did you know that Jesus went to the Feast of Tabernacles in secret? Halfway through the feast he went to the temple courts and began to teach. On the last and greatest day of the festival, Jesus stood and said in a loud voice, "Let anyone who is thirsty come to me and drink. Whoever believes in me, as the Scripture has said, rivers of living water will flow from within them" (John 7:37–38). Whether he said this during the water ceremony or not, we don't know, but surely it was fresh on everyone's minds.

Some said, "He is the Messiah!" Others were skeptical. "How can the Christ come from Galilee? Isn't he supposed to come from Bethlehem?"

Well, of course he was born in Bethlehem, but he grew up in Galilee, which was prophesied about, too. Isaiah said that Galilee would be honored when a "great light" (9:2) would dawn there.

Jesus is that light, and he told them just that! Shortly after the feast Jesus declared, "I am the Light of the World. Whoever follows me will never walk in darkness, but will have the light of life" (John 8:12). Jesus was greater than even the spectacular lightshow of the Feast of Tabernacles that lit up the city of Jerusalem. He was the Light of the World! He was the glory of God in human form.

Not long after this, Jesus met a blind man. He said to him, "While I am in the world, I am the light of the world" (John 9:5). Then he spit on the ground, made some mud, and put it on the man's eyes. "Go wash in the Pool of Siloam," he said (9:7).

The man obeyed and was healed. The Light of the World allowed this man to see light for the very first time.

When we come to Jesus, we get to be bearers of light. We get to be a glowing city on a hill that cannot be hidden as we do good deeds, bringing glory to God. And one day we will get to heaven, where the Light of the World will bring light to the whole city, and streams of living water will flow from the throne. And those days will be a forever party, greater than even the greatest day of the Feast of Tabernacles, for we will be with God.

# REFLECT

1. Name the three major parts of the Feast of Tabernacles in Jesus's day and how he fulfills all three parts.

2. What does it mean that Jesus is the Light? See Isaiah 9:2 and 1 John 1:5–7.

3. What does it mean that we are the light? See Matthew 5:14–16.

4. What does heaven not need and why? See Revelation 22:5.

---

BIBLE REFERENCE JOHN 7:1–15, 37–44; 8:12; 9:1–12

KEY VERSE JOHN 8:12

# JESUS IS THE I AM

"Very truly I tell you," Jesus answered,
"before Abraham was born, I am!"

JOHN 8:58

hings were starting to get heated. After Jesus spoke at the Feast of Tabernacles, the people were divided in their opinion of him. Some thought he was the great prophet they were expecting. Others thought he was the Christ and put their faith in him. The religious leaders, however, were getting angry. No one had ever talked like this before—saying he was bread and wanting people to eat his flesh? Saying he was going somewhere where they couldn't find him and couldn't go? Where was that? Telling them they weren't Abraham's children? That their father was actually the devil? Crazy!

"You're demon-possessed!" they said.

"I am not possessed by a demon," said Jesus, "but I honor my Father and you dishonor me. I am not seeking glory for myself; but there is one who seeks it, and he is the judge. Very truly I tell you, whoever obeys my word will never see death" (John 8:49–51).

Never see death? "Now we know you are demon-possessed!" they said. "Everyone dies, even Abraham! Are you greater than Abraham? Who do you think you are?" (John 8:52–53, paraphrase).

Jesus replied, "If I glorify myself, my glory means nothing. My Father, whom you claim as your God, is the one who glorifies me. Though you do not know him, I know him. If I said I did not, I would be a liar like you, but I do know him and obey his word. Your father Abraham rejoiced at the thought of seeing my day; he saw it and was glad" (John 8:54–56).

*Further proof that he is a lunatic*, they thought. "You are not yet fifty years old," they said, "and you have seen Abraham!" (John 8:57).

"Very truly I tell you," Jesus answered, "before Abraham was born, I am!" (John 8:58).

Now this made them really furious, and they picked up stones to throw at him, but Jesus quickly slipped away.

You might be wondering why they got so angry so fast. Of all the things Jesus said, this didn't seem the craziest. And even if he was crazy, did he deserve to be stoned?

The key to understanding this is in two little, but very important, words: I AM.

Do you remember where you've heard these words before? It comes from the story of Moses and the burning bush. God is talking to Moses, telling him to go to Pharaoh and bring the Israelites out of Egypt. Moses is fearful, and he asks God an important question: "Suppose I go to the Israelites and say to them, 'The God of your fathers has sent me to you,' and they ask me, 'What is his name?' Then what shall I tell them?" (Exodus 3:13).

God answered Moses, "I AM WHO I AM. This is what you are to say to the Israelites: 'I AM has sent me to you'" (Exodus 3:14).

The Jews knew the Scriptures very well, and they knew exactly what Jesus was saying. Jesus didn't say, "Before Abraham was born, I *was*." He could have, but he didn't. He specifically said, "Before Abraham was born, I *am*." In other words, Jesus was saying "I am the eternal one. I am equal with God. I AM GOD."

In their minds, this was blasphemy, worthy of death. And indeed it would have been blasphemy if he'd been lying. But it was the truth.

Jesus was God. Jesus IS God. Jesus always has been God. Jesus is the I AM.

## REFLECT

1. Why did the people want to stone Jesus?

2. What does the name "I AM" tell us about the character of God? And of Jesus?

3. In Hebrew, "I AM" is Yahweh, and is translated "the LORD" in our Bibles. Do some research as a family to discover how the Jewish people treated the Lord's name. Were they allowed to speak it? Write it?

---

BIBLE REFERENCE EXODUS 3:13–14; JOHN 8:48–59

KEY VERSE JOHN 8:58

# JESUS IS THE GOOD SHEPHERD

---

*"I am the good shepherd.
The good shepherd lays down his life for the sheep."*

JOHN 10:11

**I**n our last story, we heard how the crowd was quite divided on their opinion of Jesus, despite what the religious leaders thought about him. Was he telling the truth, or was he crazy? In the next chapter of John, we see Jesus do another miracle, and again, the crowd is divided.

Remember the blind man Jesus healed? The one he told he was the Light of the World? The man obeyed Jesus, washing in the Pool of Siloam, and he was healed. He could see for the very first time!

You might think, *What a happy ending to this man's story!* But it wasn't the ending. The Pharisees were upset and decided to investigate, questioning both the man and his parents, and treating them very poorly in the process. The Pharisees were angry, and they took it out on this poor man and his family. When the man refused to agree with them, they threw him out.

Jesus found the man and said, "Do you believe in the Son of Man?" (John 9:35).

"Who is he, sir?" the man asked. "Tell me so that I may

117

believe in him" (9:36).

Jesus said, "You have now seen him; in fact, he is the one speaking with you" (9:37).

Then the man said, "Lord, I believe," and he worshiped him (9:38). Both his eyes and heart were open to Jesus. He was seeing Jesus clearer and clearer.

Jesus said, "For judgment I have come into this world, so that the blind will see and those who see will become blind" (9:39).

The Pharisees had been listening, and they asked, "What? Are we blind too?" (9:40).

Jesus said, "If you were blind, you would not be guilty of sin; but now that you claim you can see, your guilt remains. Very truly I tell you Pharisees, anyone who does not enter the sheep pen by the gate, but climbs in by some other way, is a thief and a robber" (9:41–10:1).

At first this may seem confusing, but let's try to understand.[6] Unlike the man who had just been healed, the Pharisees were blind to spiritual truth. They claimed to be experts, claimed to know the truth, claimed to be the leaders and shepherds of God's people, but they didn't believe in Jesus, the One sent by God. They didn't see Jesus clearly like the man who had been healed. Jesus compares them to sheep thieves. The sheep, including this man who had just been healed, were running away from them, as well they should! True sheep follow the voice of the shepherd, not a stranger.

The Pharisees didn't understand, but Jesus continued to teach the lesson, and I'm so glad he did.

Jesus said, "Very truly I tell you, I am the gate for the sheep. . . . whoever enters through me will be saved" (10:7, 9). Jesus is our only way to safe pasture, and the only way to eternal life.

How is this possible? How does Jesus give us eternal life?

Jesus went on to explain: "I am the good shepherd. The good shepherd lays down his life for the sheep" (10:11).

He was going to die! He'd already given up so much, and now he was going to give his very life.

But there's more. Jesus explained to the people that he not only had authority to lay down his life, but to take it up again. In other words, he would rise!

*There he goes again with the crazy talk!*, they thought. "He's demon-possessed and raving mad! Why listen to him?" (10:20).

But others disagreed: "These are not the sayings of a man possessed by a demon. Can a demon open the eyes of the blind?" (John 10:21).

What do you think? Are your eyes open? If Jesus is

your Good Shepherd, you are safe with him. Listen to his voice, worship him, and let him care for you. He will lead you to good pasture and abundant life.

# REFLECT

1. What are the two "I am" statements Jesus makes in this story?

2. Read Psalm 23. How does God as our Good Shepherd care for us?
No doubt the Pharisees knew this psalm, and it probably further made them angry that Jesus was giving himself a title that was equated with God.

3. How is the promised ruler from Bethlehem described in Micah 5:2–5?

4. What is one way Jesus will appear when he comes again? See 1 Peter 5:4.

5. What two roles does Jesus play in Revelation 7:17?

---

BIBLE REFERENCE JOHN 9:1-10:21

KEY VERSE JOHN 10:11

DAY
31

# JESUS IS THE RESURRECTION AND THE LIFE

"Jesus said, 'I am the resurrection and the life. The one who believes in me will live, even though they die; and whoever lives by believing in me will never die. Do you believe this?'"

JOHN 11:25-26

ne day Jesus's dear friend Lazarus became sick. Lazarus's sisters, Mary and Martha, knew Jesus had the power to heal, so they sent for him.

Jesus got the message, but he didn't run immediately to Bethany or speak a quick word to heal Lazarus. Instead, Jesus stayed where he was for two whole days. Why did he do this? Didn't he love them?

Well, actually it was *because* he loved them that he didn't come right away.[7] He had something important to tell them and show them. Jesus said, "This sickness will not end in death. No, it is for God's glory so that God's Son may be glorified through it" (John 11:4).

When Jesus was finally ready to go, the disciples tried to stop him. Bethany was very close to Jerusalem, where the people had just tried to stone him. He would be walking into a death trap! But Jesus had a plan to teach them much about life, death, and himself, so he insisted, and plainly told them what he already knew: Lazarus was dead.

He said to them, "For your sake I am glad I was not there, so that you may believe. But let us go to him" (11:15).

Oh, how confusing life with Jesus must have been. First, he said the sickness wouldn't end in death, and now he's saying Lazarus is dead? And he wants to go? Even though Lazarus is already dead and Jesus might get himself killed? Being a disciple of Jesus was not an easy job. Thomas, bless his brave heart, said, "Let us also go, that we may die with him" (11:16).

So they went. Martha ran to meet them, saying, "Lord, if you had been here, my brother would not have died" (11:21).

Jesus replied, "Your brother will rise again" (11:23).

Martha believed in the resurrection on the last day, but she didn't understand what Jesus was about to do. Then Jesus revealed to her something really important and amazing, a clue as to what was about to happen, but also something really important for all of us. Listen carefully.

Jesus said, "I am the resurrection and the life. The one who believes in me will live, even though they die; and whoever lives by believing in me will never die. Do you believe this?" (11:25–26).

Martha answered, "Yes, Lord, I believe that you are the Messiah" (11:27).

Then Mary came and fell at Jesus's feet, crying, "Lord, if you had been here my brother would not have died" (11:32).

Jesus saw her and the mourners weeping, and became deeply moved and troubled. Maybe it was the emotion of the crowd and the helplessness of Mary and Martha. Maybe he was upset that they doubted his love for them by not coming right away, but oh, how he loved them! Or maybe it was just the ugliness of sin, death, and the thought of his own death coming so soon. So many tears were coming in the days ahead.

"Where have you laid him?" Jesus asked. And he wept.

"See how he loved him!" the people said (11:36). But others questioned him, saying, "Could he not have kept this man from dying?"

They had reached the tomb, a cave with a stone covering the entrance. "Take away the stone," Jesus said (11:39).

Martha wasn't so sure that was a good idea. It had been four days, and it was going to stink!

Then Jesus said, "Did I not tell you that if you believed, you will see the glory of God?" (11:40).

So they took away the stone. Then Jesus looked up and said, "Father, I thank you that you have heard me. I knew that you always hear me, but I said this for the benefit of the people standing here, that they may believe that you sent me." When he had said this, Jesus called in a loud voice, "Lazarus, come out!" (11:41–43).

Lazarus came out, wrapped in his grave clothes. He was alive!

Jesus allowed Lazarus to die and then raised him because he loves us and wants us to believe. He is the Resurrection and the Life! The resurrection of Lazarus is a preview of our own resurrection. Just as Jesus told Martha, if we believe in him, we will live even though we die. Like Lazarus, we too will be resurrected.

The question Jesus asked Martha is for us as well—Do you believe this?

# REFLECT

1. Who does Jesus say he is in this story?

2. It was a common belief in the time of Jesus that a person's soul hovered near the body for three days before departing. How many days was Lazarus dead, and what does this tell us? See John 11:39.

3. We learn in verses 33 and 38 that Jesus was deeply moved in spirit and troubled, and in verse 35 that Jesus wept. What emotions do you think Jesus was experiencing and why? Discuss this as a family.

BIBLE REFERENCE JOHN 11:1-44

KEY VERSE JOHN 11:25-26

# JESUS IS
# OUR TRIUMPHANT
# KING

---

They took palm branches and went out to meet him, shouting, "Hosanna!"
"Blessed is he who comes in the name of the Lord!" "Blessed is the king of Israel!"

JOHN 12:13

t was time for the Passover feast, when the Jews remembered their slavery in Egypt and God's amazing rescue. Everyone was required to go, so they all packed their overnight bags and headed to Jerusalem. Little did they know how special this particular Passover was going to be. All the Passovers they had ever celebrated were pointing to this one, and Jesus would be the final Passover lamb.

Even though the crowds didn't know all that would happen to Jesus, everyone was talking about him. The news that Jesus had raised Lazarus from the dead was spreading, and people wanted to see this great teacher and healer. Meanwhile, the Pharisees and priests were plotting to kill Jesus. They envied his popularity and saw him as a threat to their authority. They also worried what would happen if the Romans caught wind of all this, so they ordered that anyone who knew where Jesus was should report it so they could arrest him.

Jesus, of course, knew all this because he's God. And he wasn't surprised either. He knew his time to die was coming soon, and he went up to Jerusalem willingly. When they arrived at the Mount of Olives outside the city, Jesus sent two of his disciples to a nearby village to find a donkey and her colt who were tied there. "Bring them to me," he said. "If anyone says anything to you, say that that the Lord needs them" (Matthew 21:2–3).

The disciples hurried to obey. They put their cloaks on the colt, and Jesus sat on them. A large crowd gathered, and they too took off their cloaks, placing them on the road to make a royal path for Jesus. This was how a king traditionally entered a city, so by doing this the people were saying, "Yes, Jesus, be our king!" Others cut palm branches from the trees to spread on the road and to wave in celebration.

The people shouted, "Hosanna!" which means, "Lord, save us!"

The crowd grew as some went ahead and more followed shouting, "Hosanna to the Son of David!" "Blessed is he who comes in the name of the Lord! Blessed is the king of Israel!" (Matthew 21:9; John 12:13).

It was a big "Hooray for Jesus!" moment. Was it time for Jesus to become king and save them from the Romans? The crowd was buzzing with excitement and they carried their joy into the city. Everyone wanted to know who Jesus was and what all the fuss was about.

Then Jesus entered the temple and drove out all who were buying and selling there. The blind and lame came to him, and he healed them. Children continued to follow him, still shouting, "Hosanna!" All this made the chief priests and teachers angry.

"Do you hear what these children are saying?" they asked Jesus (Matthew 21:16).

"Yes," Jesus replied, "have you never read, 'From the lips of children and infants You, Lord, have ordained praise'?" (21:16).

Jesus was quoting from Psalm 8. In doing so he silenced his enemies (what could they say?) and confirmed that the children were doing the right thing (which surely infuriated them more!). The children were praising him, which is right and good, because he is God! And yes, he had come to save them!

It wasn't until after the resurrection that the disciples understood everything that had happened that day. They had assisted Jesus in fulfilling a prophecy of Zechariah: "Rejoice greatly, Daughter Zion! Shout, Daughter Jerusalem! See, your king comes to you, righteous and victorious, lowly and riding on a donkey, on a colt, the foal of a donkey" (9:9). Jesus was their king, coming to bring salvation and peace. He wasn't coming to drive out the Romans, as they may have expected, but he was coming to bring them salvation and victory through his death and resurrection so we can have peace with God.

We now know this day as Palm Sunday, and we know

Jesus as our reigning king. For the Jews, this was the day they would choose their lamb for the sacrifice. They would select a one-year-old male, without defect. Jesus presented himself to the people by riding into Jerusalem on a donkey. It was as if he was saying, "Here I am. I'm your perfect lamb. I'm your Messiah and your king. Will you choose me?"

# REFLECT

1. Why do you think Jesus came on a donkey rather than a horse, which was more typical for a king? How does Zechariah 9:9 describe the king?

2. Find a picture of a donkey's back. What do you notice?

3. Read Psalm 24:7–10 and picture Jesus entering Jerusalem.

4. Read the prophecy in Zechariah 9:9–10. Is Jesus just the king of the Jews?

5. Read Revelation 7:9–10. When will people wave palm branches again? What will they say?

6. Read Revelation 19:11–16. What is Jesus riding in this passage? Why do you think it has changed?

---

**BIBLE REFERENCE** MATTHEW 21:1-17; JOHN 12:12-19

**KEY VERSE** JOHN 12:13

# JESUS IS THE WAY, THE TRUTH, AND THE LIFE

Jesus answered, "I am the way and the truth and the life.
No one comes to the Father except through me."

JOHN 14:6

ust a few days later it was time for the feast of the Passover. Tension was rising in the city and Jesus knew the time had come for him to die. He loved his disciples very much, but soon he would have to leave them. It would be in his leaving, in his dying, that he would ultimately be with them forever.

Jesus asked his disciples to prepare for the Passover, which they gladly did. They'd been celebrating the Passover since they were children, and knew all the traditions well, but this year would be so much different.

When they were all at the table, Jesus said to them, "I have eagerly desired to eat this Passover with you before I suffer. For I tell you, I will not eat it again until it finds fulfillment in the kingdom of God" (Luke 22:15–16).

Then he took the cup, and when he had given thanks he said, "Take this and divide it among you. For I tell you I will not drink again from the fruit of the vine until the kingdom of God comes" (22:17–18).

Then Jesus took the bread, gave thanks, and broke it.

He said, "This is my body given for you; do this in remembrance of me" (22:19).

He did the same thing with the cup, saying, "This cup is the new covenant in my blood, which is poured out for you" (22:20).

You have to wonder what the disciples were thinking. What was this new covenant? Why was he talking about his body and his blood? And what kingdom was he talking about?

And then Jesus started talking about one of them betraying him. What was happening?

Judas left the room, and Jesus again started talking about leaving them. "Lord, where are you going?" Peter asked (John 13:36a).

Jesus answered, "Where I am going you cannot follow now, but you will follow later" (13:36b). Then Jesus predicted that Peter would deny him three times before the night was over.

The room was stirring with questions and confusion. Jesus loved his disciples so much! And they had such a short time left.

Jesus began to explain that yes, he was leaving, but he was preparing a place for them in his Father's house.

And he would take them to be with him. "You know the way to the place where I am going," he said (14:4).

Thomas spoke what everyone else was probably thinking. "Lord, we do not know where you are going, so how can we know the way?" (14:5).

Jesus answered, "I am the way and the truth and the life. No one comes to the Father except through me" (14:6).

Yes, Jesus was leaving them, but he wanted to be with them! In fact, he *had* to leave them so he could be with them forever in his Father's kingdom. Jesus had to become the Passover lamb. It was only through his body and his blood that they could ever join him in his forever kingdom. Yes, one day they would celebrate the Passover together again. Jesus, the Worthy Lamb, would drink the cup in celebration, surrounded by his disciples and people from every tribe and nation and kingdom (Revelation 5:9–10; 19:9). It would be the ultimate Passover feast.

Through his death on the cross, Jesus became the way to the Father. Jesus is the Way, he is the Truth, and he is the Life. Do you want to come to the Father? Do you want to be at that feast? Jesus is the Way.

# REFLECT

1. What does the Old Testament Passover look back to? What does the New Testament Passover (the Lord's Supper) look back to? How are they related?

2. How is Jesus the Way? How is he the Truth? How is he the Life?

3. Jesus told the disciples that he is the Way, the Truth, and the Life during a time when they were very troubled. What is troubling you today, and how might this knowledge help you?

4. As a family, research Jewish Passover celebrations. What are the four cups of the celebration, and what might this add to our understanding? What is the *afikomen*, and how might it point to Jesus?

---

**BIBLE REFERENCE** LUKE 22:7–23; JOHN 13:31–14:7

**KEY VERSE** JOHN 14:6

# JESUS IS THE TRUE VINE

"I am the vine; you are the branches.
If you remain in me and I in you, you will bear much
fruit; apart from me you can do nothing."

JOHN 15:5

esus packed in a ton of teaching that final night with his disciples. He spoke with actions by washing their feet and breaking bread with them. He spoke of the future, predicting his betrayal, Peter's denial, and the suffering and grief the disciples would experience in the coming days and years. He spoke promises of the Holy Spirit, saying it was good for them that he was going away, so that the Counselor, the Spirit, could come. And he spoke to them again in parables.

Jesus said to them, "I am the true vine, and my Father is the gardener" (John 15:1).

The metaphor of a vine was not a new idea for the disciples. Many times in the Old Testament, Israel is compared to a vine or vineyard. In Isaiah 5:1–7 we learn of a well-loved vineyard, planted on a fertile hillside. God took care of the vineyard perfectly, clearing the land, planting the best vines, and guarding it with a watchtower. The vineyard, however, produced only bad, sour fruit. So the vineyard was destroyed.

Israel was the vine, and Israel had failed. The disciples knew this.

But now Jesus was saying something different to them. Israel was no longer the vine; *he* was! Israel had failed to produce good fruit—they had majorly messed up. But Jesus was perfect. Where Israel had failed, Jesus had succeeded. The disciples couldn't rely on belonging to Israel to be saved. They needed to belong to Jesus, the True Vine.

Jesus said, "Remain in me, as I also remain in you. No branch can bear fruit by itself; it must remain in the vine. Neither can you bear fruit unless you remain in me" (John 15:4).

The Old Testament prophets dreamt of the day when Israel would "bud and blossom and fill all the world with fruit" (Isaiah 27:6). Because of Jesus, this can happen! All of us have the opportunity to abide in Jesus and bear fruit for the glory of God. Bearing fruit is the purpose of the vineyard, and now it's our purpose, too.

Jesus makes it clear that we cannot bear fruit by ourselves. We must be attached to him, the vine. God as the gardener prunes us to make us even more fruitful. If we obey him, bear fruit, and love one another, we will be filled with joy. And he will even call us his friends.

Knowing what would happen so soon, Jesus said, "Greater love has no one than this: to lay down one's life for one's friends" (15:13). The very next day Jesus would die on the cross, taking on the judgment that belonged to Israel, to us, and to the whole world.

Israel had failed. We, as sinful people, have failed. Without him we can do nothing. But Jesus, the True Vine, stepped into the world to accomplish what we could not. When we remain in him, we receive everything we need to live and to bear fruit that will last.

# REFLECT

1. Who was the vine in the Old Testament? And who is the vine now?

2. What does it mean to remain (or abide) in the vine?

3. How can you bear fruit?

4. Why does a gardener prune a vine? Why and how does God prune us?

5. What was the very first command God gave to Adam and Eve? See Genesis 1:28.

---

**BIBLE REFERENCE** JOHN 15:1-17

**KEY VERSE** JOHN 15:5

# JESUS IS THE SUFFERING SERVANT

He was despised and rejected by mankind, a man of suffering, and familiar with pain.

ISAIAH 53:3A

t's no surprise that our next story is the crucifixion. This story, along with the resurrection, is the heart of the gospel, and what all our other stories have been pointing towards. Without the crucifixion and resurrection there would be no salvation, no hope for sinners. Jesus had to suffer to save us.

But to the people of Jesus's day, it was a surprise. You might remember a conversation Jesus had with Peter. Jesus explained that he must suffer many things at the hands of the elders, chief priests, and teachers of the law, and that he must be killed, and on the third day be raised to life.

Did Peter say, "Yes, Lord! That's the plan!"?

No, instead Peter rebuked Jesus. "Never, Lord!" he said, "This shall never happen to you!" (Matthew 16:22).

The disciples didn't understand that Jesus had to suffer. It didn't make sense to them. To them the promised Messiah was an exalted king who was powerful, mighty, and victorious, not someone who would suffer a humiliating death.

And yet it was all there in the Scriptures. Isaiah speaks of a Suffering Servant. He wrote, "He was despised and rejected by mankind, a man of suffering, and familiar with pain. . . . Surely he took up our pain and bore our suffering, yet we considered him punished by God, stricken by him, and afflicted. But he was pierced for our transgressions, he was crushed for our iniquities; the punishment that brought us peace was on him, and by his wounds we are healed" (Isaiah 53:3–5).

And Jesus did indeed suffer. He was betrayed by Judas, and the rest of the disciples deserted him and fled. He was ridiculed, slapped, and spat upon. They put on him a purple robe and a crown of thorns, mocking him as the "King of the Jews." They gave him a staff and pretended to kneel before him, and then they took the staff and hit him with it again and again. They then led him outside the city to crucify him, forcing him to carry his own cross. Jesus was crucified alongside two criminals. The soldiers divided his garments and cast lots for his clothing. Jesus cried out, "My God, my God, why have you forsaken me?" (Matthew 27:46b). Then darkness came over the land, the curtain in the temple was torn in two, and Jesus gave up his spirit. The earth shook and the rocks split. Tombs broke open and dead were raised to life. The centurion guarding Jesus was terrified and exclaimed, "Surely he was the Son of God!" (27:54).

Suffering was God's plan for his Son from the beginning. When Isaiah speaks of the Suffering Servant, he writes, "He will be raised and lifted up and highly exalted" (Isaiah 52:13).

It seems a strange thing to us, hard to wrap our minds around, but when Jesus was lifted up on that cross with the nails in his hands and feet, humiliated and suffering beyond our comprehension, he was highly, highly exalted! By suffering for unworthy sinners like you and me, the glory of God's grace was displayed for all to see. It's a scene that will make God's people rejoice for eternity.

We can see this so clearly when we read of the Lamb in the book of Revelation. The Lamb is Jesus, and what does he look like? He's a lamb that's been slain (5:6)! And everyone is worshiping the Lamb *because* he was slain! It is in his suffering that he is exalted and we are healed.[8]

We can join with the saints, singing, "You are worthy to take the scroll and to open its seals, because you were slain, and with your blood you purchased for God persons from every tribe and language and people and nation. You have made them to be a kingdom and priests to serve our God, and they will reign on the earth" (Revelation 5:9–10).

Jesus, the Lamb of God, suffered and died for me and for you. He is the final Passover Lamb, slaughtered for us. He took on the suffering and punishment that we deserved, and by his wounds we are healed.

# REFLECT

1. In what ways did Jesus suffer for us?

2. Was there ever a day when more prophecies were fulfilled than the day that Jesus died? If time permits, explore a list of prophecies concerning Jesus's death that were fulfilled on Good Friday.

3. God's plan to save us through his Son's suffering and death was not an afterthought. It was planned before the Creation of the world. What is the full name of the book of life? See Revelation 13:8, ESV.

---

**BIBLE REFERENCE** MATTHEW 27:27–54; REVELATION 5:1–14

**KEY VERSE** ISAIAH 53:3A

# JESUS IS THE FIRSTFRUITS

---

*But Christ has indeed been raised from the dead, the firstfruits of those who have fallen asleep.*

1 CORINTHIANS 15:20

fter Jesus suffered and died, he was taken down from the cross by a man named Joseph of Arimathea. Normally the bodies of crucified criminals were left unburied and not given much care, but Joseph courageously asked for Jesus's body and placed him in Joseph's own new tomb, cut from rock. The women who had stayed with Jesus at the cross went with Joseph to lay him to rest, and then went home to prepare spices and perfumes for his body. The next day was Saturday, their Sabbath, and they rested.

Meanwhile, the chief priests and Pharisees decided they didn't want any more drama surrounding Jesus. Jesus had said he would rise, and they didn't want to take any chances with someone stealing his body and pretending he was alive. So they made the tomb extra secure by putting a seal on the stone and placing guards on duty in front of it.

On Sunday morning, the women took their spices and went to the tomb. To their surprise, the heavy stone had been rolled away and the body was missing! Suddenly glowing angels appeared. The women were scared and bowed down with their faces to the ground.

But the angels said to them, "Why do you look for the living among the dead? He is not here; he has risen!" (Luke 24:5–6).

The women hurried away, afraid, but full of joy, and ran to tell the disciples the amazing news! The disciples, however, did not believe them, thinking it was nonsense—impossible! But Peter and John had to know. They got up and ran to the tomb. Peter bent over the place where Jesus's body had lain, saw the strips of linen, and wondered to himself. Then John also came in, and he saw and believed.

Jesus, their dear friend and Lord, was alive! Oh, there was so much they still didn't understand, but he was alive! That evening the disciples were together, locked in a room because they were afraid of the Jewish leaders. Suddenly Jesus came and stood with them, and said, "Peace be with you!" (John 20:19). Then he showed them his pierced hands and side. It was really him!

How did Jesus get in the room if the door was locked? Did he walk through the walls like he had walked out of his grave clothes? Maybe, but the Bible doesn't tell us. We do know that he had a physical body, because the disciples could see him and touch him, and later they ate fish with him. But clearly there was something different about him.

The difference is that Jesus no longer had a mortal body. He would never die again (Romans 6:9). But there's more. The Bible tells us that Jesus is the "firstfruits of those who have fallen asleep" (1 Corinthians 15:20). It sounds important, but what does it mean?

In the Old Testament God commanded the people to celebrate the Feast of Firstfruits. It was celebrated during the beginning of the harvest, and the people were commanded to bring the first part of their harvest to the Lord. Often it was barley, and the people would bring it to the priests and offer it as a wave offering before the Lord. In doing this they were saying, "God, you've provided this, the beginning of the harvest, and we trust that you will provide the rest of it, abundantly!"

Jesus is the Firstfruits because he was the first to rise. We can look to him and say, "Yes, Lord, we trust that we will rise too! We will have a body just like your resurrected body!"

Many Bible scholars believe that first Easter Sunday was also the Feast of Firstfruits. As the people of God were bringing their firstfruits to the temple that day, Jesus the Firstfruits was rising, giving us hope and confidence in our own resurrection. Jesus has risen, and if you believe in him, so will you!

# REFLECT

1. Why is the resurrection of Jesus so important? See 1 Corinthians 15:17.

2. What hope does the resurrection give you?

3. Read 1 Corinthians 15:20-23 and try to explain the concept of firstfruits in your own words. See Leviticus 23:9-20 if you would like to read more about the Feast of Firstfruits.

4. What do you think our resurrected bodies will be like?
See Philippians 3:20-21 and 1 Corinthians 15:49.

---

**BIBLE REFERENCE** LUKE 23:50-24:12; JOHN 20:3-9, 19-20

**KEY VERSE** 1 CORINTHIANS 15:20

# JESUS IS THE SON OF MAN

*"From now on you will see the Son of Man sitting at the right hand of the Mighty One and coming on the clouds of heaven."*

MATTHEW 26:64

e've learned a lot of names for Jesus over the last few weeks, but we haven't talked about the name Jesus most often used for himself. Do you know what it is? Jesus called himself the Son of Man. In fact, he used it more than eighty times in the Gospels, so we should pay attention!

At first glance this name is quite simple, and something very few people would argue with. He was the son of a human, an ordinary girl named Mary. He was fully man—someone who needed food and water to survive, probably got sick or hurt, and was tired when he went to bed. He was a person, a son of man, just like you and me.

But this name also has a deeper meaning—a meaning that Jesus surely understood when he chose to call himself by this name. It comes from a prophecy in the book of Daniel.

Daniel had a frightening dream in which four great beasts rose up out of the sea. The first was like a lion with the wings of an eagle, the second like a hungry bear, the third like a winged leopard, and the fourth was just plain scary. It had iron teeth, ten horns, and was trampling and devouring everything in sight. And then came another little horn—boastful and with eyes like a man's. While Daniel watched, the beast was slain, and its body was thrown into the fire. It was pretty scary stuff, and when Daniel learned the meaning of it, he turned pale. These were kingdoms and kings that would rule on earth. Kingdoms opposed to God, which would be allowed to rule for a time.

But then came the good news. Daniel saw God, the Ancient of Days, wearing white and seated on a fiery throne. Then came "one like a son of man, coming with the clouds of heaven. He approached the Ancient of Days and was led into his presence. He was given authority, glory and sovereign power; all nations and peoples of every language worshiped him. His dominion is an everlasting dominion that will not pass away, and his kingdom is one that will never be destroyed" (Daniel 7:13–14).

This Son of Man in Daniel's dream is the ultimate power and the ultimate authority. His rule will never end. Never.

When Jesus called himself the Son of Man, he was identifying himself with the man in this vision. He *is* the man in this vision. Sure, the Romans were in power during his time on earth, but they wouldn't be

forever. No earthly power lasts forever. Jesus was going to take his place on the throne of the only kingdom that will last forever.

And that's exactly what he did when he ascended into heaven. Forty days after his resurrection, Jesus took the disciples to the Mount of Olives. They asked him, "Lord, are you at this time going to restore the kingdom to Israel?" (Acts 1:6).

Jesus said to them, "It is not for you to know the times or dates the Father has set by his own authority. But you will receive power when the Holy Spirit comes on you; and you will be my witnesses in Jerusalem, and in all Judea and Samaria, and to the ends of the earth" (Acts 1:7–8).

And just like that, he was taken up into heaven in a cloud. You might think this would make them sad. Jesus wasn't going to overthrow the Romans right away, and even worse, he was leaving them! But the Bible doesn't say they were sad. No! They were filled with joy! Why? Because Jesus went to heaven! In a cloud! Just like the Son of Man in Daniel! He was on his throne that very minute! His rule was starting *now!*[9]

And they knew they would see him again. Two angels appeared and told them that Jesus would come back in the same way they saw him go. Jesus himself had said this at his trial. When asked if he was the Christ,

Jesus answered, "You have said so. But I say to all of you: From now on you will see the Son of Man sitting at the right hand of the Mighty One and coming on the clouds of heaven" (Matthew 26:64).

Jesus, the Son of Man, is on his throne. His place at the right hand of God is a place of power and authority. He has been exalted, and the kingdom of God is here!

# REFLECT

1. What are the two meanings of the name "Son of Man"?

2. Read the following verses: Mark 8:31; 9:31; and 10:33-34. What does Jesus say will happen to the Son of Man?

3. Have you ever tried to picture the moment Jesus was reunited with his Father in heaven? Take a minute to imagine it.

4. Recite the Apostles' Creed together, emphasizing the phrase, *"He ascended into heaven and is seated at the right hand of God the Father Almighty."*

5. Why is it important to remember Jesus is on his throne *right now*?

BIBLE REFERENCE DANIEL 7:13-14; LUKE 24:50-53; ACTS 1:6-11

KEY VERSE MATTHEW 26:64

# JESUS IS
# THE SENDER OF
# THE SPIRIT

---

*"But very truly I tell you, it is for your good that I am going away. Unless I go away, the Advocate [Spirit] will not come to you; but if I go, I will send him to you."*

JOHN 16:7

The disciples were waiting. Jesus had told them to stay in Jerusalem until the promised gift of the Spirit came, and you can bet they were excited. Jesus had promised them power with the Holy Spirit, and that they would be his witnesses in Jerusalem, Judea, Samaria, and all the way to the ends of the earth. How would it happen? What would it look like? Feel like? And when would it come? You can imagine their anticipation.

The city was bustling with Jewish pilgrims from all over the world. They had come for the Feast of Weeks, also known as the Feast of Harvest or the Feast of Dedication. It was a time of celebration and thanking the Lord for the gift of the harvest, the gift of food in abundance!

The Jews had added more to the celebration, also making it a time to thank God for the gift of the Law.[10] The feast started fifty days after Passover, which was about the time they were first given the law at Mount Sinai, so the timing made sense. Do you remember the story? It's a dramatic one—the mountain was wrapped in smoke and the Lord came down in fire. The whole mountain shook and the sound of trumpets and thunder grew louder and louder. Then Moses went up and received the Ten Commandments. God was making the Israelites his treasured possession and into a kingdom of priests, who by obeying him were to be different from the other nations. Through them the world would see what it looks like when God is in charge. But when Moses came down the mountain after his special meeting with God, he found the people worshiping that awful golden calf, and that day about 3,000 men died as punishment. Moses went back up the mountain and received new tablets, and the Lord renewed the covenant. Then Moses came down with his face shining because he had been in the presence of the Lord, which was an incredibly special thing.

Now we fast-forward to the celebration of the law and the harvest, the Feast of Weeks. Today we call it by its Greek name, Pentecost, which means fiftieth. It was on this day that the disciples were all gathered together in one room, waiting for the gift Jesus had promised them. Suddenly there came from heaven a sound like a rushing wind, and it filled the entire house where they were sitting. And if that wasn't dramatic enough, tongues of fire appeared, dividing and resting on each of them. They were all filled with the Holy Spirit and began to speak in different languages—languages they had not known before!

God was making them a kingdom of priests again, only this time they had God's Spirit inside them. The fire of God's presence on Mount Sinai was now a tongue of fire on their heads and coming into their hearts. They each had God's Spirit and could carry this power with them wherever they went. God's presence was not limited to the mountain or the temple any longer.[11]

Hearing the commotion, a crowd gathered, and each one heard the disciples speaking of the wonders of God in their own language. They were amazed! "What does this mean?" they asked (Acts 2:12).

Peter stood and addressed the crowd. He explained that what was happening was spoken by the prophet Joel many years before. God's Spirit would now be poured out on all believers. And he told them pretty bluntly that the same Jesus whom they had crucified was now sitting at the right hand of God. The people felt awful and wondered what they should do. Peter told them, "Repent and be baptized, every one of you, in the name of Jesus Christ for the forgiveness of your sins. And you will receive the gift of the Holy Spirit" (Acts 2:38).

And so on that day 3,000 people believed and were baptized. And these people, from many different languages and nations, were filled with the Spirit, and would begin to carry the good news of Jesus to the world.

Pentecost, which began as a celebration of God's abundant harvest, would now be a celebration of the abundance of the Spirit. And God's Spirit would travel in the hearts of his people, his priests, to the nations of the world until the day of God's final harvest.

# REFLECT

1. Why do you think God chose this particular time to send the Spirit? Who was in Jerusalem at the time?

2. Name all the Bible stories you can think of where God reveals himself in the form of fire.

3. How many parallels can you find between the giving of the law at Sinai and the giving of the Spirit at Pentecost?

4. The law of God is called the Torah in Hebrew, meaning *teaching*. What did Jesus say the Holy Spirit would do in John 14:26?

---

**BIBLE REFERENCE** ACTS 2:1-13

**KEY VERSE** JOHN 16:7

# JESUS IS THE LAST ADAM

So it is written: "The first man Adam became a living
being"; the last Adam, a life-giving spirit.

1 CORINTHIANS 15:45

s we've traveled through the Bible over
the last few weeks, we've read so many
stories that point us to Jesus. Isn't the
Bible amazing? God's plan to redeem his
people has been in place since the beginning. It was
not an afterthought or a "Plan B" after Adam and Eve
messed up. It was always God's plan to bring us to himself through his Son.

Even Adam, way back in Genesis, points us to Jesus
Christ. In fact, the apostle Paul calls Jesus the "Last
Adam." He says, "'The first man Adam became a
living being'; the last Adam, a life-giving spirit" (1
Corinthians 15:45).

When we picture Adam in Genesis, we often picture
him surrounded by animals—a giraffe, a lion, a deer,
and maybe a curious monkey or parrot on his shoulder.  And when we picture baby Jesus, we often picture
a few sheep, and maybe a donkey or a cow, all crowding around a manger. Both Adam and Jesus were surrounded by the creatures of God on their first earthly
day. But there are other similarities too.

Adam was the beginning for the human race; and Christ is our new beginning, our new hope. Adam was the first ruler over creation, and Jesus is the ultimate ruler over creation.

You see, Jesus is *like* Adam, but *way better* than Adam. One very big difference is that Jesus never sinned. Oh, he was tempted as Adam was, but he never sinned. Being fully human, fully God, and totally perfect qualified Jesus to reverse the curse we inherited through Adam.

We are connected to both Adam and Jesus. We are connected to Adam through our humanity and our sin, and we are connected to Jesus through our faith and his grace. The Bible even says that we are adopted into the family of God when we believe (Ephesians 1:5). We're not just sons and daughters of Adam and Eve, but sons and daughters of God as well.

As children of God, one day we will live with new bodies on the new earth. God will make everything new. It will be like the perfect paradise Adam and Eve experienced in the garden, but even better! Heaven and earth will be joined, and we will worship together around the throne. And like Adam in Eden, and Jesus by the manger, animals will be there![12]

Revelation 5:13 says, "Then I heard every creature in heaven [maybe eagles and hummingbirds] and on earth [maybe dogs and porcupines] and under the earth [maybe moles and hedgehogs] and on the sea [maybe whales and stingrays], and all that is in them, saying: 'To him who sits on the throne and to the Lamb be praise and honor and glory and power, for ever and ever!'" (Revelation 5:13, with additions).[13]

What an incredible sight that will be! Thanks be to Jesus, the Last Adam, for making it possible for us to join him in paradise for all eternity.

# REFLECT

1. What are some similarities between Adam and Jesus?

2. What are some differences between Adam and Jesus?

3. How do you picture the garden of Eden? How do you picture the new earth?

4. In Genesis God commanded Adam to rule over creation. What will we do on the new earth? See Revelation 22:1-5 (answer is in 5b) or Revelation 5:10.

---

**BIBLE REFERENCE** 1 CORINTHIANS 15:20-23, 45-49

**KEY VERSE** 1 CORINTHIANS 15:45

# JESUS
# IS THE
# BRIDEGROOM

*"Let us rejoice and be glad and give him glory! For the wedding of the Lamb has come, and his bride has made herself ready."*

REVELATION 19:7

 e've come to our last day, but still we have not studied all the names of Jesus, prophecies about Jesus, or stories that point to him. The Bible is an amazing book, full of valuable treasures for us to discover. Let's uncover one last important picture of Jesus today.

In the book of Revelation, the final book of the Bible, Jesus is pictured as a bridegroom at a wedding feast. Nowadays we usually shorten *bridegroom* to just *groom*—the man getting married—so the picture is of Jesus celebrating his own marriage. At the same time

Jesus is pictured as a lamb, which might make it even more confusing for you, but remember the picture of the lamb helps us think of Jesus's sacrifice. And who is his bride? His bride is the church. In other words, his bride is US.

At first this sounds really strange, but if we take the time to dig and think a little bit, we'll find a beautiful picture of God's love for us, his church.

It helps to know a little bit about the marriage customs of Jewish people. Most marriages during Bible times were arranged. In other words, the father would pick a bride for his son. He and the bride's father would agree on a bride price, or dowry, and they would sign a contract. The contract was a promise, and it was binding. This was like an engagement today, only it couldn't be broken off easily. At this point the groom would go home to his father's house and start building on to the house to make a place for himself and his future wife. Once he was done and the father approved of the home, he would send his son to get the bride. Meanwhile the bride was to spend time getting her wedding clothes ready. She didn't know exactly when the groom would come for her, so she just had to be ready. Often the groom would come at night to surprise his bride, and his friends would run ahead to announce his arrival. "Here's the bridegroom! Come out to meet him!" (Matthew 25:6).

Then it was time for the wedding, and following the wedding, a feast! Wedding feasts in Bible times often lasted a week. God's people knew how sacred and special marriage was, and they loved to celebrate it!

Before God the Father even created the world, he picked you to be part of the bride of Christ (Ephesians 1:4). Then he made a covenant with his people, much like signing a contract, and he promised to pay the very costly bride price. The price would be the blood of his own Son, but God determined the bride was worth it! Jesus told his disciples that following his death and

resurrection, he would go back to his Father's house to prepare a place for them (John 14:2–3), just like a Jewish groom would prepare a place for his bride, and he's preparing a place for you too! Your job right now is to prepare your wedding garments, which the book of Revelation tells us are the "righteous deeds of the saints" (Revelation 19:8 ESV). (*Saints* is just a fancy word for someone who believes in Jesus.) One day, when God the Father says the time has come (Matthew 24:36), Jesus will return to claim his bride. We need to be ready, because we don't know when it will happen! We will hear the sound of the trumpet, meet the Lord in the air, and at last become his bride (1 Thessalonians 4:16–17). And then finally we will feast at a party more amazing than we could possibly imagine.

The idea of marriage might feel strange to you right now, but remember it's a picture, not an exact description. Just like a husband loves his wife and would give up anything for her, Jesus loves us and gave himself up for us. This is what Jesus accomplished that first Easter. Because of Easter, we will enjoy an incredibly close relationship with Jesus forever. Our bridegroom paid the ultimate price for us—his own life! And then he rose from the grave, crushing sin and death so we can live in his Father's house with him forever.

And that, friends, is what we celebrate on Easter morning—and something we can celebrate every day. Jesus is risen! He is risen indeed!

# REFLECT

1. How is Jesus our bridegroom?

2. How does it make you feel to know Jesus is preparing a place for you right now?

3. Read Revelation 19:8. What are the bride's wedding clothes, and how are you preparing yours?

4. How do you picture Jesus's second coming? See 1 Thessalonians 4:13-18.

5. How do you picture the wedding supper of the Lamb? See Revelation 19:4-9.

6. Take some time to read through the symbols and the names of Jesus from the last forty days. Then pray together, thanking God for who Jesus is and what he has done for us.

---

BIBLE REFERENCE JOHN 14:1-4; REVELATION 19:4-9

KEY VERSE REVELATION 19:7

# "REFLECT"
# ANSWERS
# AND SONG
# SUGGESTIONS

## 1: JESUS IS THE FIRSTBORN OVER ALL CREATION

1. The Father, Son, and Holy Spirit were all present at creation.
2. Day 1: light and dark; Day 2: sky separated from water; Day 3: dry land; Day 4: sun, moon, and stars; Day 5: birds and fish; Day 6: land animals and people.
3. Jesus *is* the image of God, and we *reflect* the image of God. This means we are not God, but are like him in many ways. We can do all sorts of things animals cannot (speaking, reading, praying, thinking complexly, having emotions, creating, etc.). And we are relational, like God, and he desires a relationship with us!
4. Answers will vary.
5. Jesus is exalted over all creation. All things are created by him, through him, and for him, and he holds all things together.

"Creation Sings the Father's Song," Keith and Kristyn Getty, Stuart Townend
"All Things Together," Andrew Peterson
"Jesus Christ Is the Same," Randall Goodgame
"Mystery," Todd Smith, Angela Smith (Selah)
"Across the Lands," Keith and Kristyn Getty

## 2: JESUS IS THE SERPENT CRUSHER

1. Sin entered the world through Adam, and death through sin—in this way, death came to all people, because all sinned.
2. Sin separates us from God. The wages of sin is death.
3. Jesus is the serpent crusher!

"Nothing but the Blood of Jesus," Robert Lowry
"Grace Greater Than Our Sin," Julia H. Johnston
"For God So Loved the World," Randall Goodgame
"Christ Is Risen," Matt Maher

## 3: JESUS IS THE ARK AND THE DOOR

1. Jesus delivers us from judgment, just as the ark did for Noah. We can only be saved if we are "in Christ." He's the perfect ark!
2. Jesus is the door or gate to salvation. Whoever enters through him will be saved.
3. God has "set his bow in the cloud." He's not pointing his war bow at us, but has instead hung it up, making a covenant with us and promising not to destroy us. We can perhaps even take it a step further, noticing that with the bow in this position, the arrow is pointing at heaven.
4. Rainbows are in heaven around God's throne. This makes sense because the rainbow is a reminder to God of his covenant to not destroy us. We do not need to fear his judgment for our sin because God is remembering his covenant. He has provided a way for us to enter heaven through Jesus.

5. God will not send another worldwide flood, destroying all living creatures. God will deal with sin in a new way, through sacrifice.

"God Rescues Noah from the Storm," Sally Lloyd-Jones, Flo Paris (Rain for Roots)
"Great Is Thy Faithfulness," Thomas O. Chisholm

## 4: JESUS IS THE ONE THROUGH WHOM THE WORLD IS BLESSED

1. Abram means "exalted father"; Abraham means "father of many."
2. God responds to a man's faith by giving (crediting) righteousness to him. See also Galatians 3:6–7.
3. God took all the responsibility for keeping the covenant. Abram could never keep this covenant on his own, and neither can we!
4. Answers will vary.

"Father Abraham," traditional children's song
"By Faith," Stuart Townend, Keith and Kristyn Getty
"Sometimes by Step," Rich Mullins

## 5: JESUS IS THE LAMB GOD HAS PROVIDED

1. Similarities include: one and only son; wood on back; mountain/hill; no struggle (obedience); lamb provided; substitution.
2. God did not spare his own Son as he spared Isaac.
3. Answers will vary.
4. Abraham named the place "The Lord Will Provide." God provided a lamb as a substitute for Isaac, and he provided his Son Jesus as

the lamb in our place. This place, Moriah, was also where the temple was built, where many lambs were sacrificed for sins, and is also near the place where Jesus was crucified.

"Behold the Lamb of God,"
Andrew Peterson
"My Faith Looks Up to Thee," Ray Palmer
"Hallelujah for the Cross," Ross King
"Just as I Am, without One Plea," Charlotte Elliott
"Christ the True and Better," Matt Boswell, Keith Getty, Matt Papa

## 6: JESUS IS THE STAIRWAY TO HEAVEN

1. There is only one way to heaven—through Jesus!
2. Jesus is our only way to heaven.
3. Answers will vary.
4. Answers will vary.

"Come Thou Fount of Every Blessing," Robert Robinson
"Nearer My God to Thee," Sarah Flower Adams
"I Love to Tell the Story," Kate Hankey, William Fischer
"Heavenly Sunlight," Henry Zelley

## 7: JESUS IS THE BETRAYED AND THE SAVIOR

1. Similarities include: leaving his home and father; brothers not believing him; wanted dead; betrayed for silver; punished though innocent; and the saving of many lives.
2. Answers will vary.
3. Jesus comes from the line of Judah; Jesus offers his life in our place.

"Wonderful, Merciful Savior,"

Dawn Rodgers, Eric Wyse
"In All Things," Randall Goodgame
"My Savior's Love," Charles H. Gabriel
"Beautiful Savior," Joseph Seiss

## 8: JESUS IS THE DELIVERER

1. Answers may include: prince stepping down to save his dearly loved people from slavery; shepherd; in Egypt until God called him out; deliverer; time in the desert; and promised land
2. Answers may include the grave, death (Hosea 13:14), evil (Matthew 6:13), or this present evil age (Galatians 1:4).
3. We found over eighty results in our search! God wanted to remind his people over and over again how he had rescued them, not only so they would love and obey him, but also to point them to Jesus's deliverance from sin and death.
4. Answers will vary.

"Guide Me, O Thou Great Jehovah," William Williams
"My Deliverer Is Coming," Rich Mullins
"Christ the True and Better," Matt Boswell, Keith Getty, Matt Papa

## 9: JESUS IS THE PASSOVER LAMB

1. Some Egyptian gods include Ra/Re (the sun god), Osiris (god of death), Heqt (frog goddess for childbirth), Apis (bull god), Nut (sky goddess), and Set (god of desert storms). A simple internet search will produce a variety of answers. It's also interesting to note that the pharaoh and his firstborn son were considered to be gods as well.
2. Jesus was sinless, without "blemish or defect."
3. It is called the Passover because God literally passed over the homes of

the Israelites and did not kill them.
4. Jesus's blood was "poured out for many for the forgiveness of sins" (Matthew 26:28).

"Passover Us," Andrew Peterson
"Behold the Lamb (Communion Hymn)," Keith and Kristyn Getty, Stuart Townend
"Redeemed, How I Love to Proclaim It," Fanny Crosby

## 10: JESUS IS THE ROCK MOSES STRUCK

1. Answers may include: saved them from the Egyptian army; pillar of cloud and pillar of fire; water and manna; ultimately saving them through Christ.
2. Jesus was pierced and water flowed from his side. The punishment that brought us peace was upon *him*.
3. Answers will vary.
4. Answers will vary.

"Rock of Ages," Augustus Toplady
"There Is a Fountain Filled with Blood," William Cowper
"Jesus Keep Me Near the Cross," Fanny Crosby
"Christ Our Hope in Life and Death," Jordan Kauflin, Keith Getty, Matt Boswell, Matt Merker, Matt Papa

## 11: JESUS IS THE MEDIATOR

1. He spoke to God on behalf of the people, pleading for them.
2. Jesus goes between us and God. He speaks to the Father in our defense. He reconciles us to God through his blood on the cross.
3. Jesus is our access to God. Through his blood on the cross, we can come to God.

"Abide with Me," Henry Francis Lyte
"Blessed Redeemer," Avis B. Christiansen, Casting Crowns
"Plead for Me," Sovereign Grace Music
"A Face That Shone," Michael Card

## 12: JESUS IS THE TABERNACLE

1. God was present with his people through the tabernacle, cloud, and fire.
2. God is present with us today through the Holy Spirit.
3. Altar—sacrifices; basin—cleansing; table of the bread of the presence—bread representing the twelve tribes; lampstand—light; altar of incense—sweet-smelling smoke; ark of the covenant—God's Presence rested here.
4. The curtain was torn in two from top to bottom. We now have access to God through the blood of Jesus; we can enter his Presence any time.
5. It is a cube. There is no tabernacle or temple because the Lord God Almighty and the Lamb are its temple.

"Holy, Holy, Holy," Reginald Heber
"Better Is One Day," Matt Redman
"In the Beginning," Randall Goodgame

## 13: JESUS IS THE MERCY SEAT

1. The ark was a chest of pure gold with cherubim overshadowing the mercy seat, or atonement cover. It held the Ten Commandments, a jar of manna, and Aaron's staff. It was the place where God's Presence rested. The high priest would sprinkle blood on it on the Day of Atonement to pay for the people's sins.
2. Jesus is the place where we are reconciled to God. He was stained with blood. He covers our sin.
3. There are two of them, one sitting at the head and the other at the foot of where Jesus had been.
4. The sins of the people were placed on the goat. Jesus "carries our sins away" from God's Presence.

"Nothing but the Blood," Robert Lowry
"The Power of the Cross," Stuart Townend, Keith Getty
"My God How Wonderful Thou Art," Frederick William Faber

## 14: JESUS IS THE ONE WHO IS LIFTED UP

1. God sent the venomous snakes because the people were complaining and rebelling against the Lord . . . again. Yes, we complain and rebel too, probably every day!
2. The people were saved by looking at the bronze snake on the pole. We are saved when we look up to Jesus on the cross and believe.
3. He was talking about Jesus dying on the cross. The following verse is John 3:16, "For God so loved the world that he gave his one and only Son, that whoever believes in him shall not perish but have eternal life." Jesus could have allowed the people to die from the snake bites, but in his love he provided a method of salvation.

"Lift High the Cross," George Kitchin, Michael Newbolt
"Worthy Is the Lamb," Darlene Zschech
"Jesus, Keep Me Near the Cross," Fanny Crosby

## 15: JESUS IS THE STAR FROM JACOB AND THE SCEPTER FROM ISRAEL

1. The star and scepter point to Jesus. They are both royal images full of glory and authority.
2. God will use whomever he wants to use!
3. Answers will vary. Consider memorizing Numbers 23:19 to remember God is faithful to keep his promises.
4. Jesus became the curse for us.
5. Numbers 23:10 (I will make you into a great nation), Numbers 23:21 (I will be with you), Numbers 24:5–6 (give you the land), Numbers 24:7 (make you into a great nation), Numbers 24:9 (bless those who bless you)

"There Shall a Star Come out of Jacob," Felix Mendelssohn
"Glory," JJ Heller
"O Morning Star, How Fair and Bright," Philipp Nicolai, Catherine Winkworth
"Jacob's Star," Michael Card

## 16: JESUS IS OUR KINSMAN REDEEMER

1. He provided for them in the Israelite law, allowing them to glean grain.
2. He married Ruth, redeemed her property, and gave her a son.
3. Jesus is our brother. Jesus became human and died in our place, redeeming us.
4. David was Ruth's great-grandson.
5. People from all nations are in God's family.
6. Jesus was born in Bethlehem.

"Matthew's Begats," Andrew Peterson
"Redeemed, How I Love to Proclaim It," Fanny Crosby
"I Will Sing of My Redeemer," Philip P. Bliss

## 17: JESUS IS THE GREAT HIGH PRIEST

1. The priests served the Lord in the tabernacle, and later in the temple. They offered sacrifices to atone for the sins of the people.
2. Jesus was tempted in every way, yet did not sin. He can empathize with our weaknesses. He ascended into heaven and sits at the right hand of God.
3. Both Melchezidek and Jesus were king and priest.

"Before the Throne of God Above," Charitie Lees Bancroft, Vikki Cook
"Jesus, My Only Hope," Mark Altrogge
"It Was Finished Upon That Cross," CityAlight

## 18: JESUS IS THE SON OF DAVID

1. She would have a son, Jesus. He would be called the Son of the Most High. The Lord would give him the throne of his father David, and he would reign forever.
2. Similarities include: Bethlehem; shepherd; rescuer; victor over enemies; great king; and family line.
3. Jesus reigns in heaven over all things and will reign forever. He is our rescuer from sin and the victor over the enemy. Jesus is the Great Shepherd and the Prince of Peace.
4. Jacob is blessing his sons, and he says the scepter will not depart from Judah. David and Jesus are from the line of Judah.

"O Worship the King All Glorious Above," Robert Grant
"Rejoice, the Lord Is King," Charles Wesley
"He Shall Reign," Laura

Hackett Park, Ben Shive
"Once in Royal David's City," Cecil Alexander
"Come, Thou Long-Expected Jesus," Charles Wesley
"So Long, Moses," Andrew Peterson
"Christ the True and Better," Matt Boswell, Keith Getty, Matt Papa

## 19: JESUS IS OUR GREAT PROPHET

1. The job of a prophet is to speak God's message to the people, often telling them to turn back to God.
2. Jesus is fully God and eternal. All things were made through him. God sent the Word (Jesus) to us.
3. God spoke through prophets in the Old Testament, and now he speaks to us through his Son.

"In the Beginning," Randall Goodgame
"I Know That My Redeemer Lives," Samuel Medley
"Join All the Glorious Names," Isaac Watts, Bob Kauflin

## 20: JESUS IS GREATER THAN JONAH

1. Jesus and Jonah have many similarities: sleeping at the bottom of the boat; in a storm; others think they will die in it; made the waters calm; three days in the fish/tomb; came out at the Lord's command.
2. Jesus is greater than Jonah because he created and commands the sea, and he saves all who believe in him.
3. God rules the sea. This was a big clue that Jesus is God!
4. Jesus "purchased for God persons from every tribe and language and people and nation" (Revelation 5:9).

"The Lord Is My Salvation," Keith and Kristyn Getty
"This Joyful Eastertide," George Ratcliffe Woodward
"O Praise the Name (Anástasis)," Benjamin Hastings, Dean Ussher, Marty Sampson
"Jesus Stops a Storm," Sally Lloyd-Jones, Sandra McCracken, Katy Bowser (Rain for Roots)

## 21: JESUS IS THE HORN OF OUR SALVATION

1. We are weak (ESV) and powerless (NIV).
2. Jesus is strong and able to save. We are safe and secure with Jesus on our side.
3. God delivered David from the hand of all his enemies, and from the hand of Saul. Jesus has the power to keep us safe both in this life and the life to come. Even when we die, we are safe if we believe in him.

"Zechariah's Prophecy," Randall Goodgame
"A Mighty Fortress Is Our God," Martin Luther
"Guide Me O Thou Great Jehovah," William Williams
"More Than Conquerors," Rend Collective

## 22: JESUS IS THE PRINCE OF PEACE

1. Answers will vary.
2. It's hard to imagine how something perfect can increase! It may be helpful to reflect on the hymn "Like a River Glorious," which speaks of God's perfect peace growing deeper and fuller every day.

3. We are filled with the peace of God in believing (ESV) or trusting (NIV).

"Joy Has Dawned," Keith Getty, Stuart Townend
"Unto Us a Child Is Born," Randall Goodgame
"Crown Him with Many Crowns," Matthew Bridges
"Hark! The Herald Angels Sing," Charles Wesley, George Whitefield
"All Hail the Power of Jesus' Name," Edward Parronet

## 23: JESUS IS THE SON OF GOD

1. God the Father spoke, the Son was baptized, and the Holy Spirit descended like a dove.
2. God said he was pleased (delighted) with his Son, and the Spirit came on him in the form of a dove.
3. "God made him who had no sin to be sin for us, so that in him we might become the righteousness of God" (2 Corinthians 5:21).
4. Adam is called the son of God in Luke, and we too are children of God. Jesus and Adam are different in that Adam, the first man, was from the dust of the earth, and Jesus is from heaven. Adam was sinful, and Jesus is sinless.

"To God Be the Glory," Fanny Crosby
"Man of Sorrow, What a Name," Philip P. Bliss
"Before the Throne of God Above," Charitie Lees Bancroft, Vikki Cook

## 24: JESUS IS THE MIRACLE WORKER

1. Answers will vary.
2. The ceremonial washing would no longer be needed. Jesus has come, and we can be washed in his blood. Jesus is now the way to be purified.
3. Answers will vary.

"Our God," Chris Tomlin
"I Heard the Voice of Jesus Say," Horatius Bonar
"I Love to Tell the Story," Kate Hankey, William Fischer

## 25: JESUS IS THE CLEANSER

1. It's okay to be angry over sin. God has anger over sin, and God cannot sin.
2. Yeast represented sin. Jesus was on a mission to rid the world of sin.
3. Jesus cleanses us through his death on the cross. First Corinthians 6:11 says, "You were washed, you were sanctified, you were justified in the name of the Lord Jesus Christ and by the Spirit of our God."
4. Our bodies are temples of the Holy Spirit. God dwells in us, and therefore we should take care of our bodies and flee from sin.

"Whiter Than Snow," James Nicholson
"Grace Greater Than Our Sin," Julia H. Johnston
"Nothing but the Blood of Jesus," Robert Lowry

## 26: JESUS IS THE LIVING WATER

1. We can get water very easily, but for the people of the Bible, water was not always readily available, and getting it was hard work.
2. His time had not yet come to die. She was a "safer" person to reveal himself too since she was a Samaritan (not someone who had the authority to crucify him). Or perhaps it is to emphasize that people of all nations are included in God's family.
3. The river of life flows from the throne of God and of the Lamb.
4. There is no cost! It is a free gift.
5. God's voice is like the roar of rushing waters.

"Living Water," Randall Goodgame
"The Well," JJ Heller
"Living Waters," Kristyn Getty, Ed Cash
"The Goodness of Jesus," CityAlight
"God So Loved," Andrew Bergthold, Ed Cash, Franni Cash, Martin Cash, and Scott Cash

## 27: JESUS IS THE BREAD OF LIFE

1. Answers will vary.
2. We must "believe in the one he has sent" (John 6:29).
3. We are remembering and proclaiming his death, demonstrating our belief in him.
4. Passover bread is striped and pierced.

"Guide Me, O Thou Great Jehovah," William Williams
"Behold the Lamb (Communion Hymn)," Keith and Kristyn Getty, Stuart Townend

## 28: JESUS IS THE LIGHT OF THE WORLD

1. The three parts of the feast are tabernacle, light, and water. Jesus came to tabernacle (dwell) among us, he is the Light of the World, and he is the Living Water.
2. We are in darkness because of our sin, and Jesus is our light—our way out, our hope. Jesus brings us back to God, who is light.
3. We shine Jesus's light to the world by doing good deeds

and bringing glory to God.

4. Heaven does not need a lamp or the light of the sun, because God is light.

"Let Your Light Shine," Randall Goodgame

"Be Thou My Vision," Eleanor Hull, Mary Byrne

"The Light of the World Is Jesus," Philip P. Bliss

## 29: JESUS IS THE I AM

1. By saying, "Before Abraham was born, I am," he was claiming to be God. They believed this claim to be false, but it's the truth!

2. God is real, eternal, and does not change. He is self-existent, meaning that he doesn't need anything. Jesus too is real, and is the same yesterday, today, and forever. He is the image of God, and through him we can draw near to God.

3. The Jews revered God's name and would not speak it, fearing they would take the Lord's name in vain, breaking the third commandment. Instead, they would pronounce Yahweh as "Adonai." They wrote it differently too so people would remember to pronounce it that way.

"Jesus Christ Is the Same," Randall Goodgame

"Surely God Is with Us," Rich Mullins

"What Wondrous Love Is This," traditional hymn

"Before the Throne of God Above," Charitie Lees Bancroft, Vikki Cook

## 30: JESUS IS THE GOOD SHEPHERD

1. "I am the gate for the sheep,"

and "I am the good shepherd."

2. He gives us everything we need, including rest and refreshment. He comforts us and keeps us safe. He promises goodness, mercy, and an eternal dwelling.

3. He is a great and strong shepherd, known to the ends of the earth. He will bring peace.

4. Jesus will appear as the Chief Shepherd.

5. Jesus is both the Lamb and the Shepherd.

"Jesus, Tender Shepherd, Hear Me," Mary Lundy Duncan, Keith and Kristyn Getty

"Savior, Like a Shepherd Lead Us," Dorothy A. Thrupp

"The Good Shepherd," Fernando Ortega

"Yet Not I, but Through Christ in Me," CityAlight

## 31: JESUS IS THE RESURRECTION AND THE LIFE

1. Jesus is the resurrection and the life.

2. Four days—Lazarus was definitely dead!

3. Possible answers are included in the devotional, but the Scriptures do not give a certain reason.

"How Deep the Father's Love for Us," Stuart Townend

"And Can It Be," Charles Wesley

"Who Is He in Yonder Stall," Benjamin Hanby

"I Will Rise," Chris Tomlin

## 32: JESUS IS OUR TRIUMPHANT KING

1. He was a different kind of king. He was humble and obedient to death.

2. The fur on the donkey's back looks like a cross!

3. Perhaps a parent can read the question, "Who is this king of glory?" and the kids can shout the answer.

4. No, his rule will extend to the ends of the earth.

5. Before the throne of God people will wave palm branches and cry, "Salvation belongs to our God, who sits on the throne, and to the Lamb."

6. He is riding a white horse, a symbol of victory.

"To the King Sing Hosanna," Keith and Kristyn Getty

"Lead On, O King Eternal," Ernest Shurtleff

"Hosanna, Loud Hosanna," Jeanette Threlfall

## 33: JESUS IS THE WAY, THE TRUTH, AND THE LIFE

1. The OT Passover looks back to the exodus, and the NT Passover looks to the cross. They are related through deliverance, a lamb, and death "passing over."

2. Jesus is the Way to the Father, salvation, and heaven. He is the Truth in that he is trustworthy, and a firm foundation. He is the Life because he alone can save us from death.

3. Answers will vary.

4. There's some speculation and different interpretations here, but it's fascinating to study.

"I Am the Way," Randall Goodgame

"That Where I Am There You May Also Be," Rich Mullins

"Behold the Lamb (Communion Hymn)," Keith and Kristyn Getty, Stuart Townend

"To God Be the Glory," Fanny Crosby

## 34: JESUS IS THE TRUE VINE

1. Israel is the vine in the OT. Now Jesus is the vine.
2. To abide in Jesus is to have a daily, personal relationship with him.
3. We bear fruit when we abide in the vine. Our outward actions are a result of our heart and our relationship with Jesus. See Galatians 5:22–23 for the fruit of the Spirit.
4. A gardener prunes a vine to encourage more growth. God "prunes" us to make us more fruitful. He prunes as he teaches, rebukes, corrects, and trains us through his Word, knocking down our idols and drawing us closer to himself.
5. Be fruitful!

"I Am the Vine," Randall Goodgame
"Abide with Me," Henry Francis Lyte

## 35: JESUS IS THE SUFFERING SERVANT

1. He was betrayed, abandoned, falsely accused, mocked, despised, rejected, spat upon, flogged, crucified, pierced, and forsaken by God.
2. Use a study Bible or an online search to find a list of prophecies.
3. The full name is "the book of life of the Lamb who was slain."

"Man of Sorrows, What a Name," Philip Bliss
"When I Survey the Wondrous Cross," Isaac Watts
"O Sacred Head Now Wounded," Bernard of Clairvaux
"You Are the Christ," Randall Goodgame
"By His Wounds," Randall Goodgame
"Is He Worthy?" Andrew Peterson

## 36: JESUS IS THE FIRSTFRUITS

1. Jesus conquered death by rising from the grave. If Christ had not been raised, our faith would be futile.
2. We too will rise!
3. Answers will vary.
4. They will be like Jesus's glorious body.

"Christ the Lord Is Risen Today," Charles Wesley
"Low in the Grave He Lay," Robert Lowry
"Because He Lives," Bill and Gloria Gaither
"Christ Is Risen, He Is Risen Indeed," Keith and Kristyn Getty, Ed Cash
"See What a Morning," Keith Getty, Stuart Townend

## 37: JESUS IS THE SON OF MAN

1. Jesus was the child of Mary and Joseph, a son of man and fully human, but he is also the Son of Man in Daniel's vision, equal with God and reigning forever.
2. The Son of Man will suffer, be rejected by the elders, priests, and teachers, be delivered into the hands of men, mocked, spit on, flogged, killed, and rise three days later.
3. Answers will vary.
4. The Apostles' Creed can be found online and in many hymnals.
5. Jesus is in complete control right now, which can bring us great comfort and hope!

"Crown Him with Many Crowns," Matthew Bridges
"Rejoice, the Lord Is King," Charles Wesley
"Jesus Shall Reign," Isaac Watts
"Beautiful Savior," Joseph Augustus Seiss

"Jesus Came to Earth," Bob Kauflin, Dave Campbell, Solomon Campbell
"There Is a Higher Throne," Keith and Kristyn Getty

## 38: JESUS IS THE SENDER OF THE SPIRIT

1. People from many nations were gathered in Jerusalem for the feast and would spread from there, bringing the gospel with them.
2. Answers will vary.
3. Parallels include: on or near a mountain; a gift received; loud noise; fire; the number 3,000.
4. The Holy Spirit will teach us and remind us everything Jesus has said.

"When the Fullness of Time Had Come," Randall Goodgame
"Holy Spirit, Living Breath of God," Keith Getty, Stuart Townend
"Dwell in Me, O Blessed Spirit," Fanny Crosby
"Shine, Jesus, Shine," Graham Kendrick
"There Is a Redeemer," Melody Green

## 39: JESUS IS THE LAST ADAM

1. Similarities include: beginning; ruler; animals; connected to us.
2. Jesus is perfect, and Adam was sinful. Adam lost paradise, Jesus regains it.
3. Answers will vary.
4. We will reign with him!

"By the Sea of Crystal," William Kuipers
"And Can It Be?" Charles Wesley
"Come Behold the Wondrous Mystery," Matt Boswell, Michael Bleecker, Matt Papa
"Behold Our God," Jonathan Baird, Meghan Baird, Ryan